LEVEL G • GRADE 12

Integrated Performance Assessment

Teacher's Manual with Assessment Forms

Dr. Roger Farr, Director,
Center for Reading and Language Studies at Indiana University

HB Assessment Group,
a Professional Assessment Company

HOLT, RINEHART AND WINSTON
Harcourt Brace & Company
Austin • New York • Orlando • Atlanta • San Francisco • Boston • Dallas • Toronto • London

STAFF CREDITS

Project Director: Kathleen Daniel
Executive Editor: Mescal K. Evler
Managing Editor: Robert R. Hoyt
Project Editors: Richard Blake, Scott Hall, Amy Strong
Editorial Staff: Julie Barnett, Joel Bourgeois, Roger Boylan, Jeffrey T. Holt, Katherine E. Hoyt, Constance D. Israel, Carrie Laing Pickett, Atietie O. Tonwe, Michael Webb
Editorial Support Staff: Ruth A. Hooker, Roni Franki, Kelly Keeley, Margaret Sanchez, Pat Stover
Editorial Permissions: Ann Farrar
Sr. Art Director: Pun Nio
Cover Design: Bob Bretz
Interior Design: Janet Brooks, Alicia Sullivan
Packaging Design: Joe Melomo
Production Coordinator: Rose Degollado
Manufacturing Coordinator: Michael Roche

ABOUT THE AUTHOR

Dr. Roger Farr is currently Chancellor's Professor of Education and Director of the Center for Reading and Language Studies at Indiana University. He is a past president of the International Reading Association and the author of both traditional norm-referenced tests and performance assessments. Dr. Farr has taught at both elementary and high school levels in New York State and has served as a school district reading consultant.

The International Reading Association presented Dr. Farr the William S. Gray award for outstanding lifetime contributions to the teaching of reading in 1984. He was elected to the IRA Reading Hall of Fame in 1986 and was selected by the IRA as the Outstanding Teacher Educator in Reading in 1988.

ASSESSMENT DESIGN

Gene Jongsma, David Markson and Tami Steelman of HB Assessment Group

EXCERPTED MATERIALS

The following selections were excerpted from their original sources for instructional purposes:
From *Robinson Crusoe* by Daniel Defoe (page 46)
From *The Journals* by Dorothy Wordsworth (page 65)
From *Testament of Youth* by Vera Brittain (page 80)

Printed in the United States of America

ISBN 0-03-095105-4

12345 022 00 99 98 97 96

CONTENTS

INTRODUCTION TO INTEGRATED PERFORMANCE ASSESSMENT 1

Rationale for Integrated Performance Assessment 1

Features of These Integrated Performance Assessments 1

An Overview of the Assessments for Level G—Grade 12 2

Development of Integrated Performance Assessment 2

Evidence of Validity and Reliability...3

ADMINISTERING INTEGRATED PERFORMANCE ASSESSMENT 5

General Guidelines...5

Options for Administering Integrated Performance Assessment......................5

Using Collaboration When Administering Assessments..................................6

Observing Students' Communication Skills 7

Providing for Students with Special Needs 8

HOLISTIC SCORING OF INTEGRATED PERFORMANCE ASSESSMENT 9

Guidelines for Holistic Scoring 9

Scoring the Reading Section 9

General Scoring Rubric for Reading...11

Scoring the Writing Section 14

Scoring Rubrics for Writing..14

Customizing the Scoring System 14

INTERPRETING AND SHARING PERFORMANCE ASSESSMENT RESULTS 15

Sharing Results with Students..15

Sharing Results with Parents...15

Using Results to Assign Grades 16

APPENDIX

RUBRICS 18

Abbreviated Rubric for Scoring Reading...18

Scoring Rubric for Rhetorical Effectiveness in Autobiographical Incident...........19

Scoring Rubric for Speculation about Causes and Effects................................20

Scoring Rubric for Rhetorical Effectiveness in Reflective Essay 21

Scoring Rubric for Rhetorical Effectiveness in Informative Report........................22

General Rubric for Conventions 23

COPYING MASTERS OF STUDENT ASSESSMENT FORMS 25

  Assessment 1 27

    READING: Poem 28

    WRITING: Autobiographical Incident (Narrative) 38

  Assessment 2 45

    READING: Novel, excerpt 46

    WRITING: Writing: Speculation about Causes and Effects (Expository).........56

  Assessment 3 63

    READING: Poem/Journal, excerpt 64

    WRITING: Reflective Essay (Expository) 73

  Assessment 4 79

    READING: Autobiography, excerpt 80

    WRITING: Informative Report (Expository) 89

COPYING MASTERS OF CHECKLISTS 95

  Reading/Writing Observational Checklist, Part 1 96

  Reading/Writing Observational Checklist, Part 2 97

  Speaking/Listening Observational Checklist 98

MODEL PAPERS WITH ANNOTATIONS 99

  Assessment 1 101

    READING: Poem

      High 102

      Medium 108

      Low 114

    WRITING: Autobiographical Incident (Narrative)

      High 120

      Medium 123

      Low 125

  Assessment 2 127

    READING: Novel, excerpt

      High 128

      Medium 133

      Low 138

    WRITING: Speculation about Causes and Effects (Expository)

      High 143

      Medium 145

      Low 147

Assessment 3 149

    READING: Poem/Journal, excerpt

        High...150

        Medium 156

        Low..162

    WRITING: Reflective Essay (Expository)

        High...168

        Medium 171

        Low..174

Assessment 4 175

    READING: Autobiography, excerpt

        High...176

        Medium 181

        Low..186

    WRITING: Informative Report (Expository)

        High...191

        Medium 194

        Low..196

FIELD-TEST SITES 197

TO THE TEACHER
USING *INTEGRATED PERFORMANCE ASSESSMENT* WITH READING AND WRITING PROGRAMS

The design of the *Integrated Performance Assessment* program allows you to adapt it for use in a wide variety of instructional settings. Each assessment consists of a Reading section and a Writing section. The Reading section provides one or two authentic literary selections and a series of open-ended questions that are scored holistically. The Writing section provides prewriting activities and a prompt that elicits a specific form of writing, and culminates in holistic scores for both Rhetorical Effectiveness and Conventions. The Reading and Writing sections may be administered either together or independently.

The chart on the following page suggests where you might most effectively use *Integrated Performance Assessment* in each of the following textbooks.

ELEMENTS OF LITERATURE

Integrated Performance Assessment Level G— Grade 12 correlates with the instructional program of *Elements of Literature, Sixth Course.* Each assessment uses a reading selection that is thematically linked to its respective collection in the literature textbook. In addition, the selection represents a reading genre (e.g., poem, short story, folktale) that the students experience in those collections. Similarly, the writing section of the assessment evaluates the writing forms that are taught in the correlating collections.

ADVENTURES IN LITERATURE

Integrated Performance Assessment Level G — Grade 12 may be readily adapted for use with *Adventures in English Literature.* In some instances the writing form may appear in a different *Adventures* unit than the reading genre.

ELEMENTS OF WRITING

Integrated Performance Assessment Level G — Grade 12 may also be used for holistic evaluation of writing forms taught in *Elements of Writing, Complete Course.*

OTHER PROGRAMS

Integrated Performance Assessment Level G — Grade 12 is easily adapted to most reading and writing programs. If you are teaching an integrated program, you may wish to use both sections of each assessment. Or, you may use just the section appropriate to your curriculum. If you are using the Reading assessment with a program not listed on the following chart, you should check for duplication of the reading assignment in your classroom materials. In case a duplication occurs, you may want to administer the Reading assessment in this manual before teaching the selection.

Correlation Chart: Integrated Performance Assessment, Level G—Grade 12

ASSESSMENT	ELEMENTS OF LITERATURE, SIXTH COURSE	ADVENTURES IN ENGLISH LITERATURE	ELEMENTS OF WRITING, COMPLETE COURSE	READING PASSAGE (GENRE)	WRITING FORM (TASK)
1	The Anglo-Saxons: 449–1066	Unit 1 (Reading and Writing)	Chapter 4 (Writing only)	"The Wanderer" translated by Burton Raffel (Poem)	Autobiographical Incident (Narrative) • Write a letter to a friend about an incident that changed your view of yourself or someone else.
2	The Renaissance: 1485–1660	Unit 3 (Reading) Unit 6 (Writing)	Chapter 7 (Writing only)	From *Robinson Crusoe* by Daniel Defoe (Novel, excerpt)	Speculation about Causes and Effects (Expository) • Write two alternative endings for the novel and speculate as to which is better.
3	The Romantic Period: 1798–1832	Unit 4 (Reading and Writing)	Chapter 4 (Writing only)	"I Wandered Lonely as a Cloud" by William Wordsworth (Poem) & From *The Journals* by Dorothy Wordsworth (Journal, excerpt)	Reflective Essay (Expository) • Write a reflective essay for the school newspaper that discusses an experience that provided new insights about growing up.
4	The Twentieth Century	Unit 6 (Reading) Unit 1 (Writing)	Chapter 6 (Writing only)	From *Testament of Youth* by Vera Brittain (Autobiography, excerpt)	Informative Report (Expository) • Write an informative report for your social science teacher about conflicting obligations.

INTEGRATED PERFORMANCE ASSESSMENT
HOLISTIC SCORING WORKSHOP

The *Holistic Scoring Workshop* is an easy-to-use tutorial program that introduces teachers to holistic scoring and provides opportunities to practice scoring actual student papers. This unique software program is directly correlated with the *Integrated Performance Assessment Teacher's Manual with Assessment Forms.* Call 1-800-225-5425 for prices. The program consists of two main sections shown in the Main Menu below.

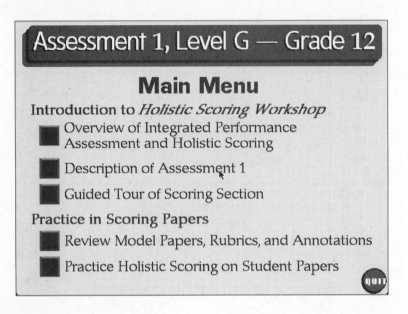

Assessment 1, Level G — Grade 12

Main Menu
Introduction to *Holistic Scoring Workshop*

■ Overview of Integrated Performance Assessment and Holistic Scoring

■ Description of Assessment 1

■ Guided Tour of Scoring Section

Practice in Scoring Papers

■ Review Model Papers, Rubrics, and Annotations

■ Practice Holistic Scoring on Student Papers

[QUIT]

- **Overview of Integrated Performance Assessment and Holistic Scoring** This section of the program introduces teachers to the basic principles of integrated performance assessment and its key feature, holistic scoring. The overview explains the rationale underlying the development of this form of assessment and offers a general introduction to holistic scoring.

- **Description of Assessment** This section previews the content of the specific assessment. It tells how to prepare for scoring reading and writing responses to that assessment and shows how to apply the rubrics to the assessment.

- **Guided Tour of Scoring Section** This section provides an annotated preview of the scoring training program.

- **Review Model Papers, Rubrics, and Annotations** This section allows teachers to try out the training program's features before entering an actual practice scoring session. In this section teachers can explore the rubrics for reading, rhetorical effectiveness, and conventions; view model student papers that illustrate high, medium, and low levels of performance; and read annotations that analyze the student papers and explain the scores that were assigned.

- **Practice Holistic Scoring on Student Papers** In this section teachers can apply what they have learned. Ten practice papers—five in reading and five in writing—are provided for each assessment. As teachers read and analyze the practice papers, they can access the rubrics, model papers, and annotations to clarify their scoring judgments. After scoring a paper, they can compare their evaluation to those of experienced scorers and read an analysis of the paper they have scored. A cumulative summary table updates and displays the percentage of agreement between the teacher's evaluation and that of an experienced scorer.

The *Holistic Scoring Workshop* is a valuable supplement to the *Integrated Performance Assessment Teacher's Manual with Assessment Forms.* The program is an ideal introduction and training tool for teachers who have little experience with holistic scoring. For more experienced teachers who may wish to refresh their holistic scoring skills, the program serves as a helpful review.

INTEGRATED PERFORMANCE ASSESSMENT

Introduction to Integrated Performance Assessment

The integrated performance assessments presented in this manual offer a unique and meaningful approach to gauging student performance. These new assessments help bridge the gap between instruction and assessment by modeling good instruction. Thus, assessment becomes a more integral part of the instructional program.

Rationale for Integrated Performance Assessment

Integrated performance assessment reflects three major trends in English education. First, many instructional programs now emphasize an integrated approach to language arts instruction—one in which reading, writing, listening, and speaking are taught in combination, not as separate subjects. Second, greater emphasis is placed on reading a variety of types of literature, some of which represent a multicultural perspective. Third, students are taught to view writing as a process in which ideas are generated, organized, revised, refined, and eventually published or shared.

The integrated performance assessments in this program were developed to

- approximate the reading, writing, speaking, and listening activities that students will encounter in most language arts programs as well as in daily life
- include a variety of reading and writing genres
- encourage students to write for different purposes and for different audiences

The following key principles guided the development of the integrated performance assessments.

➤ *Students should have opportunities to respond to a variety of types of literature.*
In the typical literature classroom students are exposed to a variety of reading materi-

als—fiction and nonfiction, poetry, plays, and many other types. The integrated performance assessments reflect this literary diversity. They capture the richness and variety in children's literature and in young adult literature.

➤ *Students should have opportunities to write for different purposes and in different modes.*
The integrated performance assessments tap a variety of writing purposes and writing modes. The writing tasks were created to reflect the types of writing many students do in the classroom as well as the types of writing found in many state and district assessments. Each assessment presents a unique writing task.

➤ *Periodically teachers should have students respond to a "standard" reading and writing task.*
An effective English education program gives students choices—both in what they read and in what they write. However, from time to time it is also useful, for purposes of evaluation, to have all students respond to the same task, or assessment. The four assessments in this manual may be used for quarterly assessment or may be administered whenever the teacher desires to check performance.

Features of these Integrated Performance Assessments

➤ *They model good instruction.*
The assessments are like "mini-lessons." By eliciting reading responses and modeling the writing process they provide instructional value.

➤ *They use authentic literature.*
Each assessment is based on a selected piece of published literature with a different theme for each selection. Some of the assessments use complete short stories and poems; others use excerpts from longer works such as novels and plays.

Many of the reading selections were written by well-known authors.

➤ *They encourage process writing.*
The assessments guide students through the process of generating and organizing their ideas. Students are given an opportunity to revise their initial drafts and create published works.

➤ *They permit collaboration.*
An optional collaborative activity is included in the writing section of the integrated performance assessments. If the

teacher desires, students can share their writing plans with classmates to gather reactions and suggestions for improving their writing.

➤ *They are diagnostic.*
By collecting students' prewriting notes and preliminary drafts, teachers can gain valuable insights into the reading, writing, and thinking strategies that students are using. The optional Speaking/Listening Observational Checklist and Reading/Writing Observational Checklist can also identify strengths and weaknesses in students.

➤ *They are flexible.*
No strict time limits are imposed, and students are encouraged to proceed at their own rate within the class time allocated for the assessment.

➤ *They are scored holistically.*
Students' responses to the reading selection are scored holistically. Likewise, responses to the writing prompt are scored holistically for rhetorical effectiveness and conventions. Thus, the integrated performance assessments offer a comprehensive view of student performance.

AN OVERVIEW OF THE ASSESSMENTS FOR LEVEL G—GRADE 12

Four assessments or prompts have been developed for use at Level G—Grade 12. The following table summarizes the characteristics of each of these assessments.

Integrated Performance Assessments for Level G—Grade 12

ASSESSMENT FORM	READING PASSAGE (GENRE)	WRITING FORM (TASK)
1	"The Wanderer" translated by Burton Raffel (Poem)	Autobiographical Incident (Narrative) • Write a letter to a friend about an incident that changed your view of yourself or someone else.
2	From *Robinson Crusoe* by Daniel Defoe (Novel, excerpt)	Speculation about Causes and Effects (Expository) • Write two alternative endings for the novel and speculate as to which is better.
3	"I Wandered Lonely as a Cloud" by William Wordsworth (Poem) & From *The Journals* by Dorothy Wordsworth (Journal, excerpt)	Reflective Essay (Expository) • Write a reflective essay for your school newspaper that discusses an experience that provided new insights about growing up.
4	From *Testament of Youth* by Vera Brittain (Autobiography, excerpt)	Informative Report (Expository) • Write an informative report for your social science teacher about conflicting obligations.

DEVELOPMENT OF INTEGRATED PERFORMANCE ASSESSMENT

The integrated performance assessments in this program were developed in collaboration with Dr. Roger Farr and the Center for Reading and Language Studies at Indiana University. This Center was chosen because of its wide range of experience in developing and scoring performance tasks. Development of the assessments took place over an extended period and involved several stages. Each major stage in that developmental process is briefly described below.

1. **Identify eligible reading genre and themes, and eligible writing forms.** In order to create assessments that actually evaluate what is taught in most literature programs, it was necessary to identify the specific reading themes and genre, and the specific writing forms and tasks that could be used at each grade level.

2. **Select an appropriate format and scoring system.** A review was made of performance assessments cited in the professional literature, as well as those used in state testing programs. Comparisons were made among the available models, and desirable features were identified. Holistic scoring was chosen as the primary method of scoring.

3. **Identify potential literature selections to use in the assessments.** Several factors influenced the selection of reading passages. First, it was important to include pieces that represented a multicultural perspective. Second, the passages had to be interesting and engaging to students. And third, they had to be of appropriate difficulty and length.

4. **Identify field-test sites.** Each assessment was field tested and evaluated with students before it was selected for publication. The field-test sites represented a variety of geographic locations and district sizes and involved diverse student populations. A list of field-test sites can be found in the Appendix.

5. **Conduct field tests of the assessments.** Field tests were conducted in the fall of 1994 and the spring of 1995 in a number of school districts across the United States. Field-test versions of the assessments were distributed to participating teachers. Teachers administered the assessments following directions very similar to those included in this manual. After completing the assessments, teachers and students evaluated them through survey questionnaires. The questionnaires addressed topics such as the appropriateness of the reading selections, student interest in the selections, the appropriateness of the writing task, student interest in the writing task, and the clarity of the questions and directions.

6. **Analyze the field test results.** For analysis, all student papers and questionnaires were returned to the Center for Reading and Language Studies. Teams of experienced readers scored the student responses to each prompt and reviewed the questionnaire results. Based on the data that were collected, judgments were made as to which prompts were working well and were engaging to students. At this point, some assessments were rejected and replaced with new ones or modified and sent out for additional field testing; others were accepted as suitable.

7. **Select the model or benchmark papers.** After the assessments to be published were selected, the total pool of student papers for each one was reviewed by a panel of judges who selected model papers to illustrate various score points. Annotations were then written for each model paper explaining and justifying the score it was given. The model papers and annotations are in the Appendix of this manual.

The entire developmental process was comprehensive and thorough. It gave the publisher a firsthand look at how students and teachers reacted to integrated performance assessment, and an opportunity to drop or correct assessments that were not working as expected.

EVIDENCE OF VALIDITY AND RELIABILITY

A test or assessment that is not valid and reliable is of little value. It is important for an assessment to measure what it claims to measure, and for it to do so consistently.

➤ *Validity*
The validity of an assessment is judged relative to the purpose for which it will be used. To answer the question, "Is this test valid?", one must first ask "for what purpose?" For example, a test that assesses knowledge of the alphabet could be extremely valid in predicting success in early reading, but not valid in predicting success in graduate school. The integrated performance assessments presented in this work were designed for the purpose of evaluating a student's ability to compre-

hend and interpret literature, and to write effectively. Therefore, they must be evaluated in light of these purposes.

As part of the field tests, teachers and students independently judged the validity of the assessment they took part in. They rated the quality of the assessment in terms of how well it measures reading ability, writing ability, thinking ability, and group communication.

The results show that teachers and students viewed the integrated performance assessments as valid measures of reading, writing, thinking, and communicating. The overwhelming majority of teachers and students thought the assessments measured reading, writing, and thinking "very well" or "well." It is interesting to note that students perceived these assessments as valid measures as often as teachers did.

➤ *Reliability*

Reliability refers to consistency in scoring. If two readers scored the same paper independently, would they assign it the same score? Data collected during the scoring process showed that readers were in exact agreement 60 to 70 percent of the time; differed by one score point 25 to 35 percent of the time; and differed by two or more points 5 percent of the time or less. These results applied to all three scales that are used in the integrated performance assessments. These results are consistent with those reported in the research literature for similar types of holistic scoring.

ADMINISTERING INTEGRATED PERFORMANCE ASSESSMENT

The integrated performance assessments in this manual may represent a new type of testing for some teachers. Unlike many traditional forms of testing, integrated performance assessment does not use standardized directions for administering and does not impose specific time limits on students. Teachers should feel free to alter the directions for administering the assessment to suit their students as well as local conditions.

GENERAL GUIDELINES

1. **Be interactive.** The assessments are a dynamic form of measurement. That means that you can, and should, interact with students while they are completing the activity. The basic rule of thumb is "test the way you teach."

2. **Be encouraging.** Your role in administering the assessments should be that of a coach. You should motivate, guide, prod, and encourage students to produce their best work.

3. **Be supportive.** You may assist students who need help. The amount of assistance you provide can range from very little to quite a bit, depending on the needs and abilities of your students. If students are unfamiliar with this type of activity, you may need to offer more guidance on the first few assessments that students complete. However, as students become more familiar with the process, you should encourage greater independence.

4. **Be clear.** The directions for administering are not standardized. If necessary, you should paraphrase the directions for students. The goal is to communicate clearly to students the nature of the task and what they are to do.

5. **Be flexible.** Not all students have to proceed through the assessment at the same rate and in the same manner. On the Writing section, for example, some students may be ready to write their first drafts while others are still planning their writing.

6. **Be reflective.** Whenever possible, encourage students to engage in self-evaluation. The Writing section of each assessment contains a set of questions intended to encourage students to judge their own work. Peer conferences may also be used to foster self-evaluation.

7. **Be fair.** Allow students adequate time to do their best work. It would be unfair to set high expectations for students and then not give them enough time to fulfill those expectations.

OPTIONS FOR ADMINISTERING INTEGRATED PERFORMANCE ASSESSMENT

These integrated performance assessments have been designed to offer teachers maximum flexibility in time and method of administration. Each assessment is composed of two main sections — a Reading section and a Writing section. The following table displays the components of an integrated performance assessment.

INTEGRATED PERFORMANCE ASSESSMENT	
Reading Section	**Writing Section**
Getting Ready to Read Time to Read Responding to the Selection	Getting Ready to Write Sharing Your Plans with Others (Optional) Thinking About Reactions Time to Write

There are basically three options for administering the assessments. The following table summarizes the features of each option.

OPTION	PURPOSE	TIME NEEDED
Administer the Reading section only	To assess a student's ability to interpret and critically evaluate a piece of literature	Approximately one class period
Administer the Writing section only	To assess a student's ability to use a specific writing form and write effectively	Approximately one class period
Administer both the Reading section and the Writing section	To gain a comprehensive view of a student's reading and writing skills	Two to three class periods

Because all of the integrated performance assessments are structured in the same way, the following directions can be used for any of them.

Administering the Reading Section (1 class period)

STEP 1: Become familiar with the reading selection and the prompts that follow it.
STEP 2: Read the directions for the Reading section found in the student booklet aloud to the class. Paraphrase the directions if necessary and answer any questions.
STEP 3: Have students read the passage independently and respond to the prompts that follow the passage.

Administering the Writing Section (1 or 2 class periods)

STEP 1: Read the "Getting Ready to Write" part of the Writing section aloud to the class to explain the writing task.
STEP 2: Have students do their initial planning independently.
STEP 3: (Optional) Allow students to share their writing plans with classmates.
STEP 4: Encourage students to think about reactions they may have received, revise their prewriting plans, and begin drafting.
STEP 5: Decide if this is a "first-draft" assessment or a polished piece. If it is a first-draft assessment, establish a time limit (e.g., 45 minutes) and inform students when their drafts will be due. If a polished piece is the goal, extend the time by an additional session or class period, permitting students more time to revise and edit their work.

USING COLLABORATION WHEN ADMINISTERING ASSESSMENTS

Collaboration has become an important part of English language arts instruction for many teachers. Research has shown, for example, that our interpretations are often shaped and influenced by the social communities that we are a part of. Likewise, peer review and other forms of collaboration have become standard parts of process writing instruction.

If collaboration is an important part of the instructional program, it should be incorpo- rated into the assessments as well. Listed below are some suggestions as to when discussion groups could be used. The teacher could select the most appropriate point at which to use collaboration based on her or his instructional goals:
• after reading the selection
• after answering the reading response items
• after formulating some initial writing plans
• after completing a first draft

The teacher can gather additional insights about students' communication skills by systematically observing them while they work on an integrated performance assessment.

The optional **Reading/Writing Observational Checklist** is designed to be used while the students are working on an integrated performance assessment. The checklist should be used to observe an individual student or small group of students, not an entire class. Therefore, before administering an assessment, the teacher should decide which student(s) to observe. For example, the teacher may target a student who has been exhibiting difficulty in class or perhaps a small group of students who have been receiving supplemental instruction.

The **Reading/Writing Observational Checklist** is composed of two parts. **Part 1: Observing the Reading Process** lists strategies that effective readers use.

Part 2: Observing the Writing Process focuses on important aspects of the writing process, such as planning, revising, and self-evaluating. A copying master of the checklist is in the Appendix.

To use the checklist, write across the bottom of the form the names of the students you wish to observe. As students read the passage individually, walk around the classroom and monitor their efforts. By talking with students about their reading and observing their reactions, you can make inferences about the strategies they are using. Use the marking key on the form to record how consistently they use the effective reading strategies.

You may wish to use the back of the checklist to note whether the students requested assistance while reading and what kind of assistance they needed. You may also want to record other relevant observations that do not fit the categories in the checklist in this area.

The best time to use **Part 2** of the checklist **(Observing the Writing Process)** is while students are working on the Writing section of an integrated performance assessment. Circulate around the room, and observe what the students are doing. Use the marking key to record which strategies they are using and how consistently they use them.

The **Reading/Writing Observational Checklist** can be valuable in planning instruction. After you have recorded your observations, look for patterns. Are there particular strategies that students are not using? If so, these can be addressed in teacher-student conferences or in future lessons.

The optional **Speaking/Listening Observational Checklist** is also intended to be used to record observations of an individual student or a small group of students while they are working on an integrated performance assessment. It is designed to focus on positive speaking and listening behaviors. A copying master of this checklist can be found in the Appendix.

Decide in advance which students you want to observe. Then write their names in the boxes at the bottom of the checklist. You may observe speaking and listening at many points during the integrated performance assessment, depending on how much collaboration you have built into the assessment. For example, the checklist could be used to observe small group discussions following the reading phase or during the prewriting phase.

The information you gather on the **Speaking/Listening Observational Checklist** should be helpful in planning instruction. It may suggest, for example, which students need to be more involved in group discussions and which students need to focus on listening to the comments of others.

PROVIDING FOR STUDENTS WITH SPECIAL NEEDS

Many school districts are faced with the challenge of adapting instruction and assessment to meet the needs of special learners. These may be students for whom English is a second language, as well as students who are physically, emotionally, or intellectually challenged. Because the integrated performance assessments are not standardized, the procedures for administering them can be adjusted to meet the needs of special learners.

You may help students who have difficulty reading the selections independently by

- providing audiotapes of the reading selections and reading along with the narration
- pairing a less proficient reader with a more proficient reader in a buddy system and allowing the more able student to provide assistance when needed
- providing assistance (e.g., pronouncing difficult words, explaining unfamiliar concepts) upon request

- permitting students to take the reading selection home to have a parent, friend, or sibling read it to them

Teachers may help students who have difficulty responding to the writing assessments by

- encouraging them to discuss their prewriting ideas with a partner before actually starting to write
- permitting them to create an audiotape of their ideas in lieu of a written response
- allowing them to do their initial planning, drafting, revising, and editing on a computer
- giving them extra time to do their planning and drafting

Keep in mind that the more the performance assessments are modified the less reliable they may be as measures of students' *independent* reading and writing abilities.

HOLISTIC SCORING OF INTEGRATED PERFORMANCE ASSESSMENT

Each integrated performance assessment yields three scores—one for reading, and two for writing.

READING ✔	**WRITING: Rhetorical Effectiveness** ✔
	Conventions ✔

The scores, which can range from a low of 1 to a high of 6, are determined by a process of holistic scoring. That is, a student's work is gauged by the criteria specified in the scoring rubrics. Model papers are provided in the Appendix to illustrate and define the criteria embodied in the rubrics.

GENERAL GUIDELINES FOR HOLISTIC SCORING

Holistic scoring has been used for many years to evaluate writing samples. Many state writing assessments, for example, employ some form of holistic scoring. In holistic scoring, the reader takes several features into consideration—weighing and balancing strengths in one feature against weaknesses in others—to arrive at a single, overall score. Holistic scoring is generally faster to do than analytic scoring, which requires separate judgments about each of several factors or features.

SCORING THE READING SECTION

In the **Reading** section of integrated performance assessment, a student reads an authentic selection, or two shorter selections, and responds to a series of five to eight open-ended questions. The questions are not scored individually. Rather, the student's responses to all the questions are considered, and a single reading score is given for the entire section.

The questions in the Reading section have been designed to assess a student's ability to construct a personal interpretation of a text. More specifically, the questions assess four levels of response from the student.

First thoughts. This refers to a reader's initial reaction to what was read. It draws on the reader's immediate images, feelings, opinions, and memories of the text. It typically involves a consideration of the text as a whole rather than of its specific parts.

Shaping interpretations. Here the reader extends his or her first thoughts, often making links across different parts of the text to arrive at a deeper, more thoughtful understanding. The reader attempts to construct a personal interpretation of the text through activities such as identifying the theme, making analogies, speculating on the motives of characters, and exploring alternative interpretations. When shaping interpretations, the reader may return to the text to confirm or revise judgments and/or seek additional evidence. As part of this process the reader may exhibit metacognitive awareness of his or her ability to process the text.

Connecting with the text. This assessment examines the reader's ability to make associations between the text and life outside of the text. Connections may be made between the text and other readings, or between the text and other media such as plays, movies, or television programs. In making connections, the reader may apply his or her understanding of human nature to the text; may form analogies between the world of the text and his or her personal world; and may make associations between a character's life and his or her own situation. In essence, the reader strives to connect the text to personal experience.

Challenging the text. The reader must step outside of the text to challenge the text, and/or to make critical judgments of quality about parts of the text or the text as a whole. For example, the reader may make judgments of the literary quality of the text; contrast types of writing styles or genres; analyze the use of specific literary features; agree or disagree with the author's point of view; speculate on how the author might have treated the subject differently; or show aesthetic appreciation of the text.

SCORING RUBRIC FOR READING

The **General Scoring Rubric for Reading** is shown on the next several pages. This version of the rubric may be considered the unabridged version in that it provides a rather extensive description of each score point. Note that four paragraphs are included for each score point. The paragraphs correspond to the four levels of response to reading explained previously.

Because some teachers might find the General Scoring Rubric too extensive and perhaps too complex to use as a reference during actual scoring, an **Abbreviated Scoring Rubric for Reading** can be found in the **Appendix.** This abridged version summarizes the key criteria contained in the complete rubric.

General Scoring Rubric for Reading

USED FOR ALL ASSESSMENT FORMS

SCORE 1 — MINIMAL READING PERFORMANCE

The student displays minimal understanding or serious misunderstanding of the text. Responses suggest that the student is processing the text at the word or sentence level. Difficult sections of the text cause frustration and may result in efforts to abandon the text (e.g., "This is boring!" "I hate this story!" "This story doesn't make sense").

The student displays no reflective thinking either about the text or his or her ability to process it. Any attempt to make meaning is fragmented and focuses on parts of the text rather than the coherent whole. The student makes no attempt to generalize beyond the text, and responses show no evidence of meaningful engagement with the text. There is no evidence of meaningful emotional or intellectual engagement with the text.

The student displays no meaningful association between the text and other texts, other media, and/or personal experience, and is unable to recognize any relevance the text has to understanding human nature. The student displays no ability to make meaningful, critical judgments about the text, or to show aesthetic appreciation. Any evaluative comments or challenges to the author or text tend to be emotional rather than rational.

SCORE 2 — LIMITED READING PERFORMANCE

The student displays a limited or superficial understanding of the text. The responses are likely to focus on selected segments of the text rather than on the text as a whole. Text difficulties (e.g., ambiguities, contradictions) are disruptive to the reader.

The student displays little, if any, reflective thinking about the text or his or her ability to process it. Any attempt to express significant understanding of the text (e.g., theme, point of view) is simplistic and superficial. The student finds it difficult to generalize beyond the text and is more likely to settle for a literal understanding. Alternative interpretations are seldom explored. The student shows little emotional or intellectual engagement with the text.

The student displays difficulty in making associations between the text and other texts, other media, and/or personal experience. Associations that are made are superficial and lack depth of understanding. The student is likely to engage in autobiographical digressions that bear little relevance to the text and shows little, if any, awareness of how the text may contribute to one's understanding of human nature.

The student displays limited ability to evaluate the text critically and shows little, if any, aesthetic appreciation of the text. Judgments of quality tend to be emotional and/or unsupported. The student tends to accept the text without questioning ideas, and discounts or ignores the text when it violates personal experience.

SCORE 3   LITERAL READING PERFORMANCE

The student displays a plausible but simplistic understanding of the text. For the most part, the student interprets the text literally. When difficulties are encountered in the text (e.g., ambiguities, contradictions), they tend to be ignored.

The student displays little reflective thinking about the text or about his or her ability to process it. Attempts to express an understanding of the text as a whole are fairly predictable and lack original insights. The student demonstrates some engagement with the text, but this connection may be more emotional than intellectual. The student shows little willingness to revise or reshape his or her interpretation based on new evidence or new understanding.

The student may make associations between the text and other texts, other media, and/or personal experience, but the associations tend to lack depth or to be unsupported. The student is not likely to challenge the author or text, and generally accepts his or her first interpretation without exploring alternative interpretations. The student displays little awareness of how the text may contribute to an understanding of human nature.

The student displays limited ability to evaluate the text critically, and the evaluations tend not to be well supported. There is little evidence of challenging the text, questioning the author, engaging in reflective reading, or showing aesthetic appreciation.

SCORE 4   THOUGHTFUL READING PERFORMANCE

The student displays a thoughtful understanding of the whole text. Responses show evidence of using cues within the text to fill in gaps, create meaning, and differentiate between literal and figurative meanings. The student may show some ability to deal effectively with text difficulties (e.g., ambiguities, contradictions).

The student displays some reflective thinking about the text but does not exhibit the deeper interpretations of more discerning readers. The student attempts to express an understanding of the text as a whole and constructs a personal interpretation that goes beyond a literal understanding, but is reluctant to explore alternative interpretations of the text. There is some evidence of emotional and intellectual engagement with the text.

The student makes some associations between the text and other texts, other media, and/or personal experience, but the associations tend to be routine and predictable. The student displays evidence of using his or her understanding of human nature to interpret the text and displays some awareness of how the text contributes to an understanding of human nature.

The student displays some ability to evaluate the text critically, but the evaluations tend to lack original insights. There may be some evidence of questioning the author, challenging the text, engaging in reflective reading, or showing aesthetic appreciation.

SCORE 5   DISCERNING READING PERFORMANCE

The student displays a thoughtful and perceptive understanding of the whole text, but the interpretation lacks the insights of exemplary readers. Responses show evidence of high-order processing. The student deals effectively with text difficulties (e.g., ambiguities, contradictions).

The student displays reflective thinking about the text but may lack the deeper interpretations exhibited by superior readers. There is evidence of emotional and intellectual engagement with the text and a willingness to explore alternative interpretations and search for a deeper understanding. The student may exhibit an awareness of his or her ability to process the text.

The student displays associations between the text and other texts, other media, and/or personal experience, and usually supports those judgments with evidence, but the associations may not be as thoughtful as those of exemplary readers. The student uses personal knowledge to interpret the text and may arrive at a new or clarified understanding of human nature.

The student displays some sensitivity to linguistic, cultural, and psychological features of the text; makes critical evaluations of the text; and usually supports those evaluations with evidence. However, the evaluations may not be as thoughtful as those of exemplary readers. The student may challenge the text by disagreeing with or questioning the author.

SCORE 6   EXEMPLARY READING PERFORMANCE

The student displays a perceptive and insightful understanding of the whole text and an awareness of how the parts work together to create the whole. Responses exhibit higher-order processing. The student may use text difficulties (e.g., ambiguities, contradictions) as a springboard to deeper meaning.

The student displays exceptional reflective thinking about the text, expresses significant insight regarding the text as a whole (e.g., theme, point of view), generalizes beyond the text, demonstrates emotional and/or intellectual engagement with the text, and generally searches for a deeper understanding of the text.

The student displays persuasive associations between the text and other texts, other media, and/or personal experience, and supports those associations with strong and compelling evidence. The student uses personal knowledge to interpret the text and arrives at new or clarified understandings of human nature.

The student displays sensitivity to linguistic, cultural, and psychological features of the text; makes thoughtful judgments about the literary quality of the text; and supports those judgments with evidence from the text and/or personal experience. Responses show evidence that the student has engaged in reflective reading (e.g., by agreeing or disagreeing with the author and/or raising questions).

SCORING THE WRITING SECTION

The **Writing** section of the integrated performance assessment is linked to the **Reading** section in one of two ways. Most of the writing assessments are linked to the topic or theme of the reading selection. In these assessments, students may use the reading selection as a springboard for writing a piece based on prior knowledge and experience. Other writing assessments require the student to write an interpretation or evaluation of the reading selection itself. In these assessments, the writing task is more closely tied to the reading selection.

Two holistic judgments are made in scoring the student's writing—one for Rhetorical Effectiveness and one for Conventions. Each dimension is scored on a 6-point scale. Rhetorical Effectiveness assesses the student's ability to communicate using the particular features of the writing form being assessed. Conventions assesses the student's proficiency in using correct grammar, punctuation, capitalization, and spelling.

SCORING RUBRICS FOR WRITING

Rubrics are provided to guide the scoring of a student's writing. The rubrics for Rhetorical Effectiveness are specifically linked to the particular writing form that is being assessed (e.g., report of information, autobiographical incident) and will therefore vary from assessment to assessment. The rubric for Conventions remains the same for all assessments. Rubrics for scoring Rhetorical Effectiveness and Conventions can be found in the **Appendix**. Model papers are also provided in the **Appendix** to illustrate various levels of performance in both Rhetorical Effectiveness and Conventions.

In scoring a student's writing, the teacher should ask two questions. *How well did the student communicate?* and *How well did the student use the conventions of written language?* To answer the first question, the rubric for Rhetorical Effectiveness should be used. To answer the second question, the rubric for Conventions should be used. These should be independent judgments. That is, features such as misspellings and grammatical errors, which fall under the rubric of Conventions, should not influence the score given in Rhetorical Effectiveness. Likewise, features such as development and support should not influence the score given in Conventions.

CUSTOMIZING THE SCORING SYSTEM

The scoring system used for the integrated performance assessments is designed to be compatible with many state assessment programs. Therefore, a 6-point scale was selected and is used consistently across all three areas that are scored—Reading, Rhetorical Effectiveness, and Conventions.

Some teachers, however, may desire a simpler scoring method that doesn't require making subtle distinctions between score points. For those teachers, a 3-point scale might be more appropriate. It is relatively easy to make the transition from the 6-point scale provided with the integrated performance assessments to a 3-point scale for classroom use. The following graphic illustrates the relationship between the two scales.

6-POINT SCALE					
Minimal Achievement	Limited Achievement	Some Achievement	Adequate Achievement	Commendable Achievement	Exceptional Achievement
1	2	3	4	5	6

3-POINT SCALE		
Limited Achievement	Adequate Achievement	Excellent Achievement
1	2	3

In using the 3-point scale, the teacher classifies the student's performance as "limited," "adequate," or "excellent." Papers that would be 1's and 2's on the 6-point scale become 1's; papers that would be 3's and 4's become 2's; and papers that would be 5's and 6's become 3's.

INTERPRETING AND SHARING PERFORMANCE ASSESSMENT RESULTS

The integrated performance assessments can provide valuable insights into students' language arts abilities by revealing how all students performed on a common task. However, it is important that performance on the assessments be interpreted in light of other reading, writing, speaking, and listening samples that have been collected. It is the range of language arts activities that students engage in that will provide the most valid understanding of their abilities and the most useful information for planning instruction.

Three sources of information that are helpful in planning instruction can be derived from the integrated performance assessments:
- the students' final products (i.e., the cumulative reading responses and the final draft in writing)
- the students' marginal notes in reading, prewriting notes, and preliminary drafts
- observations recorded while students were working on the assessments

Scoring a student's final reading responses and final draft in writing represents a type of "product evaluation." On the other hand, reviewing margin notes, prewriting notes, preliminary drafts, and observational checklists is a type of "process evaluation." When these two approaches to assessment are combined, a more thorough and comprehensive understanding of student performance is possible.

SHARING RESULTS WITH STUDENTS

If the integrated performance assessments are presented as "informal activities" rather than tests, students will gain instructional benefit from them. Listed below are some suggestions for sharing results with students.

1. Discuss the rubrics with students. Distribute copies of the rubrics for **Reading, Rhetorical Effectiveness,** and **Conventions.** Explain how the rubric is used. Show students the standards used to judge responses. You may even want to score some anonymous papers as a group, or have students score each other's papers and discuss the criteria as they apply to those papers.

2. Make photocopies of the rubrics and use them as individual score reports. As you score each student's paper, circle your rating on the rubric, make marginal comments, and circle or highlight the parts of the rubric that apply to the student's response. Discuss the reports in conferences with students, pointing out their strengths as well as areas where they could still improve.

3. After students have completed an integrated performance assessment, share the model papers with them. Show the model papers without scores. Ask students what they like and don't like about the papers.

SHARING RESULTS WITH PARENTS

Results of the integrated performance assessments may also be shared with parents. Parents will appreciate seeing what their children can do on performance-based reading and writing tasks. Listed below are some suggestions for parent-teacher conferences.

1. Show parents the integrated performance assessment so they understand the task that their student was asked to perform.

2. Show parents the child's responses, and discuss the strengths and weaknesses of the responses. Explain the scoring rubric and how the responses were evaluated.

3. Show parents the model papers to illustrate the range in student performance that is possible on this performance task. Compare their child's paper with the model papers to help put their student's paper in perspective.

4. Explain what kinds of activities they can do at home to foster greater interest in reading and writing.

Even though instructional practices are changing and new forms of assessment are emerging, most teachers are still faced with the task of giving grades. Although many teachers would prefer not to give grades, school districts and parents often insist on numerical or letter grades. The challenge is to find thoughtful ways of matching new instructional practices and assessments with more traditional requirements.

No single test, whether it is a standardized achievement test, a performance assessment, or an open-ended test, can fully measure a student's reading and writing ability. For this reason, it is important to use multiple measures of assessment.

Integrated performance assessment offers a unique approach to assessing reading and writing, but like any other form of assessment, the process has limitations. For example, a student's reading ability is assessed here by evaluating what that student writes. However, some students may perform differently if asked to answer multiple-choice questions or to discuss a literature selection. Furthermore, the writing that students do on the integrated performance assessments is somewhat constrained by the topic and writing prompt. Some students might perform differently on self-selected topics.

Therefore, it is important for the scores obtained on integrated performance assessments not to be used as the sole determiner of a report card grade or semester grade.

Optimally, the integrated performance assessments could represent one of several factors used to determine a student's grade. Those assessments could be combined with the results of selection tests, daily work samples, class participation, self-reflections, and various writing samples collected in a portfolio. However, if the responses to the integrated performance assessments do contribute to the grade awarded for a grading period, the following table is illustrative of how holistic scores can be converted into numerical or letter grades. The ranges in the table could be adjusted depending on local needs.

Holistic Score	Letter Grade	Numerical Grade
6	A	96 – 100
5	A	90 – 95
4	B	80 – 89
3	C	70 – 79
2	D	60 – 69
1	F	59 and below

COPYING MASTERS OF STUDENT ASSESSMENT FORMS

ASSESSMENT 1

READING: Poem...28

WRITING: Autobiographical Incident (Narrative)...38

Assessment 2

READING: Novel, excerpt...46

WRITING: Speculation about Causes and Effects (Expository)....................56

Assessment 3

READING: Poem/Journal, excerpt 64

WRITING: Reflective Essay (Expository)...73

Assessment 4

READING: Autobiography, excerpt...80

WRITING: Informative Report (Expository) 89

ASSESSMENT • 1

LEVEL G

NAME _____

CLASS _____

DATE _____

INTEGRATED
PERFORMANCE ASSESSMENT
STUDENT FORMS

ASSESSMENT • 1

READING SECTION

➤ Directions:

Today you will read a poem. Then you will write about what you have read. You should write down your thoughts, questions, and opinions as you read. Your notes will help you when you write about the poem. When you finish reading, answer all of the questions about the poem until you come to the word STOP.

Getting Ready to Read

The poem you are about to read, "The Wanderer" translated by Burton Raffel, tells a sorrowful "before-and-after" story. In this ancient oral elegy from A.D. 940, a warrior relives better days and laments the loss of his relatives and his overlord.

Time to Read

The Wanderer
translated by
Burton Raffel

> My thoughts about
> what I am reading

This lonely traveler longs for grace,
For the mercy of God; grief hangs on
His heart and follows the frost-cold foam
He cuts in the sea, sailing endlessly,
5   Aimlessly, in exile. Fate has opened
A single port: memory. He sees
His kinsmen slaughtered again, and cries:
     "I've drunk too many lonely dawns,
Grey with mourning. Once there were men
10 To whom my heart could hurry, hot
With open longing. They're long since dead.
My heart has closed on itself, quietly
Learning that silence is noble and sorrow
Nothing that speech can cure. Sadness
15 Has never driven sadness off;
Fate blows hardest on a bleeding heart.
So those who thirst for glory smother
Secret weakness and longing, neither
Weep nor sigh nor listen to the sickness
20 In their souls. So I, lost and homeless,
Forced to flee the darkness that fell
On the earth and my lord.
           Leaving everything,

GO ON

Weary with winter I wandered out
25 On the frozen waves, hoping to find
A place, a people, a lord to replace
My lost ones. No one knew me, now,
No one offered comfort, allowed
Me feasting or joy. How cruel a journey
30 I've traveled, sharing my bread with sorrow
Alone, an exile in every land,
Could only be told by telling my footsteps.
For who can hear: "friendless and poor,"
And know what I've known since the long cheerful
        nights
35 When, young and yearning, with my lord I yet feasted
Most welcome of all. That warmth is dead.
He only knows who needs his lord
As I do, eager for long-missing aid;
He only knows who never sleeps
40 Without the deepest dreams of longing.
Sometimes it seems I see my lord,
Kiss and embrace him, bend my hands
And head to his knee, kneeling as though
He still sat enthroned, ruling his thanes.[1]
45 And I open my eyes, embracing the air,
And see the brown sea-billows heave,
See the sea-birds bathe, spreading
Their white-feathered wings, watch the frost
And the hail and the snow. And heavy in heart
50 I long for my lord, alone and unloved.
Sometimes it seems I see my kin
And greet them gladly, give them welcome,
The best of friends. They fade away,
Swimming soundlessly out of sight,
55 Leaving nothing.
                How loathsome become
The frozen waves to a weary heart.
        In this brief world I cannot wonder
That my mind is set on melancholy,
60 Because I never forget the fate
Of men, robbed of their riches, suddenly
Looted by death—the doom of earth,
Sent to us all by every rising
Sun. Wisdom is slow, and comes

My thoughts about
what I am reading

---

1. **thane:** a soldier or a noble who is a servant of the king or lord.

GO ON

65 But late. He who has it is patient;
  He cannot be hasty to hate or speak,
  He must be bold and yet not blind,
  Nor ever too craven, complacent, or covetous,
  Nor ready to gloat before he wins glory.
70 The man's a fool who flings his boasts
  Hotly to the heavens, heeding his spleen
  And not the better boldness of knowledge.
  What knowing man knows not the ghostly,
  Waste-like end of worldly wealth:
75 See, already the wreckage is there,
  The wind-swept walls stand far and wide,
  The storm-beaten blocks besmeared with frost,
  The mead-halls[2] crumbled, the monarchs thrown down
  And stripped of their pleasures. The proudest of
   warriors
80 Now lie by the wall: some of them war
  Destroyed; some the monstrous sea-bird
  Bore over the ocean; to some the old wolf
  Dealt out death; and for some dejected
  Followers fashioned an earth-cave coffin.
85 Thus the Maker of men lays waste
  This earth, crushing our callow mirth.
  And the work of old giants stands withered and still."

   He who these ruins rightly sees,
  And deeply considers this dark twisted life,
90 Who sagely remembers the endless slaughters
  Of a bloody past, is bound to proclaim:
   "Where is the war-steed? Where is the warrior?
    Where is his war-lord?
  Where now the feasting-places? Where now the mead-
   hall pleasures?
  Alas, bright cup! Alas, brave knight!
95 Alas, you glorious princes! All gone,
  Lost in the night, as you never had lived.
  And all that survives you a serpentine wall,
  Wondrously high, worked in strange ways.
  Mighty spears have slain these men,
100 Greedy weapons have framed their fate.
   These rocky slopes are beaten by storms,
  This earth pinned down by driving snow,
  By the horror of winter, smothering warmth
  In the shadows of night. And the north angrily

---

2. **mead-halls:** large banquest halls where feasts were served and mead, an
 alcoholic beverage, was drunk.

"The Wanderer" from *Poems from the Old English*, translated by Burton Raffel. Translation copyright © 1960, 1964 by
Burton Raffel. Reprinted by permission of **Burton Raffel.**

105 Hurls its hailstorms at our helpless heads.
    Everything earthly is evilly born,
    Firmly clutched by a fickle Fate.
    Fortune vanishes, friendship vanishes,
    Man is fleeting, woman is fleeting,
110 And all this earth rolls into emptiness."

        So says the sage in his heart, sitting alone with
            His thought.
    It's good to guard your faith, nor let your grief come
      forth.
    Until it cannot call for help, nor help but heed
    The path you've placed before it. It's good to find your
      grace
115 In God, the heavenly rock where rests our every hope.

> My thoughts about
> what I am reading

"The Wanderer" from *Poems from the Old English*, translated by Burton Raffel. Translation copyright © 1960, 1964 by Burton Raffel. Reprinted by permission of **Burton Raffel.**

Responding to the Selection

Now that you have read the poem, respond to the following items as completely as possible.

1. Take a few minutes to write down your first response to the poem.

_____

_____

_____

_____

_____

_____

_____

_____

_____

_____

_____

_____

_____

_____

_____

_____

_____

_____

_____

_____

_____

GO ON

2. As the speaker in the poem "cuts" aimlessly through the frozen seas in search of a welcoming port, he says that "Fate" offers him only one comfort—that of "memory." In the chart below, compare some of the feelings and experiences the Wanderer has as an exile to those he relives from the past.

	THE WANDERER'S PRESENT	THE WANDERER'S PAST
A		
B		
C		
D		
E		
F		

GO ON

3. How are the speaker's emotions reflected in the poem's physical setting? List at least four details of the setting and explain how they mirror the Wanderer's feelings.

	SETTING DESCRIPTION	HOW IT REFLECTS THE WANDERER'S FEELINGS
A		
B		
C		
D		
E		
F		

GO ON

4. Until it was written down by a Christian monk, "The Wanderer" was sung from memory rather than read from a page. Like *Beowulf*, "The Wanderer" is an oral elegy that harpist-bards performed for audiences in communal gathering places like the "mead–halls" mentioned in the poem.

   Imagine how the poem sounded back in A.D. 940 when sung by a bard accompanied on a harp. Then stretch your imagination a little further and describe a modern-day song which reminds you of "The Wanderer." As you describe the modern-day song, explain how it is similar to and/or different from the poem. Why does the song remind you of this poem?

_____

_____

_____

_____

_____

_____

_____

_____

_____

_____

_____

_____

_____

_____

_____

_____

_____

_____

_____

GO ON

5. Read the first two lines and the last verse (lines 111–115) of the poem. Some critics have argued that the first two lines and the last verse of "The Wanderer" were added by the Christian monk who preserved the poem in writing. Do you agree? Using specific evidence from the poem to back up your opinion, explain why you do or do not agree with these critics' argument.

_____

_____

_____

_____

_____

_____

_____

_____

_____

_____

_____

_____

_____

_____

_____

_____

_____

_____

_____

_____

_____

_____

_____

GO ON

6. Use this page to write down any additional thoughts you have about the poem. Tell
   anything else about your understanding of the poem and what it means to you.

_____

_____

_____

_____

_____

_____

_____

_____

_____

_____

_____

_____

_____

_____

_____

_____

_____

_____

_____

STOP!
DO NOT CONTINUE UNTIL INSTRUCTED
This is the end of the Reading Section

ASSESSMENT • 1

WRITING SECTION

Getting Ready to Write

You are going to write a letter to a friend about an incident you have experienced. The incident should be one that improved your outlook of yourself, of someone else, or of the world. An incident is an event that occurs within a short span of time—a few minutes, a few hours, or a day. Be sure to include details that describe the autobiographical incident and help your friend understand how this incident changed your outlook.

What incident will you write about? What details will you include about the incident? How did the incident change your view for the better? Use the chart below to list some of your ideas before you begin writing.

Incident I could write about:
Details about the incident:
How the incident improved my outlook:

GO

Sharing Your Plans With Others (Optional)

Before you begin writing, share your writing plans with some of your classmates. Using your notes, tell them about the incident you plan to write about and what you will say about that incident. If you are not sure which incident to write about, tell them about the incidents you are considering and get their reactions. Ask your classmates questions like the following:

- Have I chosen an incident that will be interesting to others?
- Have I overlooked anything important I should include about the incident?
- Have I explained how this incident changed my outlook?

Jot down reactions from your classmates in the space below.

_____

_____

_____

_____

_____

_____

_____

_____

_____

_____

_____

_____

_____

_____

You should also be prepared to give comments and suggestions about your classmates' writing plans. Try to give them honest and specific suggestions. Tell them about things they may want to delete or add. Suggest ways they can organize their ideas.

GO ON

Thinking About Reactions

Spend a few minutes thinking about the comments and suggestions your classmates gave you. Review the notes you took when you met with them. Are there any changes you should make, based on their comments? Use the space below to write down any important ideas you received from your classmates or to revise your original writing plans.

_____

_____

_____

_____

_____

_____

_____

_____

_____

_____

_____

_____

_____

_____

_____

_____

_____

_____

_____

| GO ON |

Time to Write

Assume that you are writing a letter to a friend you have not seen for some time. In your letter, relate an incident you have experienced that improved your outlook of yourself, someone else, or the world. Remember that an "incident" occurs within a short span of time—a few minutes, a few hours, or a day.

Be sure to give your autobiographical incident a beginning, middle, and end. Provide specific details (including descriptions of how things looked, felt, sounded, tasted, and smelled) that will help your friend imagine the incident and how you felt as you had the experience. After reading the letter, your friend should understand why the incident was important to you.

_____

_____

_____

_____

_____

_____

_____

_____

_____

_____

_____

_____

_____

_____

_____

_____

_____

_____

_____

_____

_____

_____

_____

_____

_____

_____

_____

_____

_____

_____

_____

_____

_____

_____

_____

_____

_____

_____

_____

_____

_____

_____

_____

_____

_____

_____

_____

_____

ASSESSMENT • 2

LEVEL G

NAME _____

CLASS _____

DATE _____

INTEGRATED
PERFORMANCE ASSESSMENT
STUDENT FORMS

ASSESSMENT • 2

READING SECTION

➤ Directions:

Today you will read passages from a novel. Then you will write about what you have read. You should write down your thoughts, questions, and opinions as you read. Your notes will help you when you write about the passages. When you finish reading, answer all of the questions about the passages until you come to the word STOP.

Getting Ready to Read

In the famous novel *Robinson Crusoe,* which was written by Daniel Defoe in 1719, a storm wrecks Crusoe's ship and only he manages to swim ashore. None of the other passengers or crew survive the shipwreck. Crusoe is marooned on the island in 1659 and lives there for the next twenty-seven years. The passages you will read contain Robinson Crusoe's reflections on his situation as a castaway on an apparently un-inhabited island.

Time to Read

Imagine the selection you are about to read is from an old journal pulled from a trunk. As you read the entries in this journal, underline clues that tell you something about the kind of person the writer was. In the margins, jot down what conclusions these clues lead you to draw about the writer's personality traits.

from *Robinson Crusoe*

by

Daniel Defoe

My thoughts about what I am reading

Crusoe Takes Stock and Becomes Comfortable

I now began to consider seriously my condition, and the circumstance I was reduced to, and I drew up the state of my affairs in writing, not so much to leave them to any that were to come after me, for I was like to have but few heirs, as to deliver my thoughts for daily poring upon them, and afflicting my mind; and as my reason began now to master my despondency, I began to comfort myself as well as I could, and to set the good against the evil, that I might have something to distinguish my case from worse, and I stated it very impartially, like debtor and creditor, the comforts I enjoyed against the miseries I suffered, thus:

Evil	Good
I am cast upon a horrible desolate island, void of all hope of recovery.	*But I am alive, and not drowned as all my ship's company was.*

GO ON

| | | |

I am singled out and separated, as it were, from all the world to be miserable.

But I am singled out too from all the ship's crew to be spared from death; and He that miraculously saved me from death, can deliver me from this condition.

I am divided from mankind, a solitaire, one banished from humane society.

But I am not starved and perishing on a barren place, affording no sustenance.

I have not clothes to cover me.

But I am in a hot climate, where if I had clothes I could hardly wear them.

I am without any defense or means to resist any violence of man or beast.

But I am cast on an island, where I see no wild beasts to hurt me, as I saw on the coast of Africa; and what if I had been shipwrecked there?

I have no soul to speak to, or relieve me.

But God wonderfully sent the ship in near enough to the shore, that I have gotten out so many necessary things as will either supply my wants, or enable me to supply myself even as long as I live.

Upon the whole, here was an undoubted testimony, that there was scarce any condition in the world so miserable, but there was something negative or something positive to be thankful for in it; and let this stand as a direction from the experience of the most miserable of all conditions in this world, that we may always find in it something to comfort our selves from, and to set in the description of good and evil, on the credit side of the account.

Having now brought my mind a little to relish my condition, and given over[1] looking out to sea to see if I could spy a ship; I say, giving over these things, I began to apply my self to accommodate my way of living, and to make things as easy to me as I could.

I have already described my habitation, which was a tent under the side of a rock, surrounded with a strong pale[2] of posts and cables, but I might now rather call it a wall, for I raised a kind of wall up against it of turfs, about two foot thick on the outside, and after some time, I think it was a year and a half, I raised rafters from it leaning to the rock, and thatched or covered it with bows of trees, and such things as I could get to keep out the rain, which I found at some times of the year very violent.

I have already observed how I brought all my goods into this pale, and into the cave which I had made behind me. But I must observe too, that at first this was a confused heap of

1. **given over:** stopped.
2. **pale:** enclosure.

GO ON

goods, which as they lay in no order, so they took up all my place, I had no room to turn myself; so I set my self to enlarge my cave and work farther into the earth, for it was a loose sandy rock, which yielded easily to the labor I bestowed on it; and so when I found I was pretty safe as to beasts of prey, I worked sideways to the right hand into the rock, and then turning to the right again, worked quite out and made me a door to come out, on the outside of my pale or fortification.

This gave me not only egress and regress, as it were a back way to my tent and to my storehouse, but gave me room to stow my goods.

And now I began to apply myself to make such necessary things as I found I most wanted, as particularly a chair and a table; for without these I was not able to enjoy the few comforts I had in the world; I could not write, or eat, or do several things with so much pleasure without a table.

So I went to work; and here I must needs observe, that as reason is the substance and original of the mathematics, so by stating and squaring everything by reason, and by making the most rational judgment of things, every man may be in time master of every mechanic art. I had never handled a tool in my life, and yet in time, by labor, application, and contrivance, I found at last that I wanted nothing but I could have made it, especially if I had had tools; however, I made abundance of things, even without tools, and some with no more tools than an adze[3] and a hatchet, which perhaps were never made that way before, and that with infinite labor. For example, if I wanted a board, I had no other way but to cut down a tree, set it on an edge before me, and hew it flat on either side with my ax, till I had brought it to be thin as a plank, and then dub it smooth with my adze. It is true, by this method I could make but one board out of a whole tree, but this I had no remedy for but patience, anymore than I had for the prodigious deal of time and labor which it took me up to make a plank or board. But my time or labor was little worth, and so it was as well employed one way as another.

However, I made me a table and a chair, as I observed above, in the first place, and this I did out of the short pieces of boards that I brought on my raft from the ship. But when I had wrought out some boards, as above, I made large shelves of the breadth of a foot and [a] half one over another, all along one side of my cave, to lay all my tools, nails, and ironwork, and in a word, to separate everything at large in their places, that I must come easily at them; I knocked pieces into the wall of the rock to hang my guns and all things that would hang up.

So that had my cave been to be seen, it looked like a general magazine of all necessary things, and I had everything so ready at my hand, that it was a great pleasure to me to

_____

3. **adze:** a chisel-like tool for cutting wood.

GO ON

see all my goods in such order, and especially to find my stock of all necessaries so great.

> My thoughts about what I am reading

And now it was when I began to keep a journal of every day's employment, for indeed at first I was in too much hurry, and not only hurry as to labor, but in too much discomposure of mind, and my journal would ha' been full of many dull things. For example, I must have said thus: "Sept. the 30th. After I got to shore and had escaped drowning, instead of being thankful to God for my deliverance, having first vomited with the great quantity of salt water which was gotten into my stomach, and recovering myself a little, I ran about the shore, wringing my hands and beating my head and face, exclaiming at my misery, and crying out; 'I was undone, undone,' 'til tired and faint I was forced to lie down on the ground to repose, but durst not sleep for fear of being devoured."

Some days after this, and after I had been on board the ship, and got all that I could out of her, yet I could not forbear getting up to the top of a little mountain and looking out to sea in hopes of seeing a ship, then fancy at a vast distance I spied a sail, please myself with the hopes of it, and then after looking steadily 'til I was almost blind, lose it quite, and sit down and weep like a child, and thus increase my misery by my folly.

But having gotten over these things in some measure, and having settled my household stuff and habitation, made me a table and a chair, and all as handsome about me as I could, I began to keep my journal. . . .

King Crusoe in the Fourteenth Year of His Reign

It would have made a stoic[4] smile to have seen me and my little family sit down to dinner; there was my majesty the prince and lord of the whole island; I had the lives of all my subjects at my absolute command; I could hang, draw,[5] give liberty, and take it away, and no rebels among all my subjects.

Then to see how like a king I dined too, all alone, attended by my servants. Poll, as if he had been my favorite, was the only person permitted to talk to me. My dog, who was now grown very old and crazy,[6] and had found no species to multiply his kind upon, sat always at my right hand, and two cats, one on one side the table, and one on the other, expecting now and then a bit from my hand, as a mark of special favor.

But these were not the two cats which I brought on shore at first, for they were both of them dead, and had been interred near my habitation by my own hand; but one of them having multiplied by I know not what kind of

---

4. **stoic:** person with much self-control, who is indifferent to both pain and pleasure.
5. **draw:** to pull out their inner organs.
6. **crazy:** weak, feeble.

creature, these were two which I had preserved tame,
whereas the rest run wild in the woods, and became indeed
troublesome to me at last; for they would often come into
my house, and plunder me too, till at last I was obliged to
shoot them, and did kill a great many; at length they left me.
With this attendance and in this plentiful manner I lived;
neither could I be said to want anything but society, and of
that, in some time after this, I was like to have too much. . . .

Crusoe Finds a Footprint

It happened one day about noon going toward my boat, I
was exceedingly surprised with the print of a man's naked
foot on the shore, which was very plain to be seen in the
sand. I stood like one thunderstruck, or as if I had seen an
apparition; I listened, I looked round me, I could hear nothing, nor see anything; I went up to a rising ground to look
farther; I went up the shore and down the shore, but it was
all one, I could see no other impression but that one. I went
to it again to see if there were any more, and to observe if it
might not be my fancy; but there was no room for that, for
there was exactly the very print of a foot, toes, heel, and
every part of a foot; how it came thither I knew not, nor
could in the least imagine. But after innumerable fluttering
thoughts, like a man perfectly confused and out of myself, I
came home to my fortification, not feeling, as we say, the
ground I went on, but terrified to the last degree, looking
behind me at every two or three steps, mistaking every bush
and tree, and fancying every stump at a distance to be a
man; nor is it possible to describe how many various shapes
affrighted imagination represented things to me in, how
many wild ideas were found every moment in my fancy,
and what strange unaccountable whimsies came into my
thoughts by the way.

When I came to my castle, for so I think I called it ever
after this, I fled into it like one pursued; whether I went over
by the ladder as first contrived, or went in at the hole in the
rock which I called a door, I cannot remember; no, nor could
I remember the next morning, for never frighted hare fled
to cover, or fox to earth, with more terror of mind than I to
this retreat.

I slept none that night; the farther I was from the occasion
of my fright, the greater my apprehensions were, which is
something contrary to the nature of such things, and especially to the usual practice of all creatures in fear: but I was
so embarrassed with my own frightful ideas of the thing,
that I formed nothing but dismal imaginations to myself,
even though I was now a great way off of it. Sometimes I
fancied it must be the devil; and reason joined in with me
upon this supposition; for how should any other thing in
human shape come into the place? Where was the vessel
that brought them? What mark was there of any other footsteps? And how was it possible a man should come there?

GO ON

Responding to the Selection

Now that you have read the novel passages, respond to the following items as completely as possible.

1. Take a few minutes to write down your first response to the passages.

_____

_____

_____

_____

_____

_____

_____

_____

_____

_____

_____

_____

_____

_____

_____

_____

_____

_____

_____

_____

_____

GO ON

2. Why do you think Crusoe starts and keeps writing in his journal?

_____

_____

_____

_____

_____

_____

_____

_____

_____

_____

_____

_____

_____

_____

_____

_____

_____

_____

_____

_____

_____

_____

_____

GO ON

3. After he is shipwrecked, Crusoe makes a list of the evil and good aspects of his situation. He concludes that "there was scarce any condition in the world so miserable, but there was something negative or something positive to be thankful for in it." Do you agree or disagree with his conclusion? Explain the reasons for your opinion.

_____

_____

_____

_____

_____

_____

_____

_____

_____

_____

_____

_____

_____

_____

_____

_____

_____

_____

_____

_____

GO ON

4. What three adjectives do you think best describe Crusoe? In the chart below, list the adjectives and then give reasons for your choices.

ADJECTIVE THAT DESCRIBES CRUSOE	REASONS THAT IT DESCRIBES CRUSOE

GO ON

5. Use this page to write down any additional thoughts you have about the passages. Tell anything else about your understanding of the selection and what it means to you.

_____

_____

_____

_____

_____

_____

_____

_____

_____

_____

_____

_____

_____

_____

_____

_____

_____

_____

_____

_____

_____

_____

_____

> **STOP!**
> **DO NOT CONTINUE UNTIL INSTRUCTED**
> **This is the end of the Reading Section**

ASSESSMENT • 2

WRITING SECTION

Getting Ready to Write

Imagine that you are Daniel Defoe and are in the process of completing the novel *Robinson Crusoe*. You have already written most of the novel, and now you must decide how to end it. Your friend and publisher, Jack Singleton, has read your unfinished novel and has given you good advice about it so far. He will be able to help you decide on an ending. You are going to write a letter to Jack Singleton that speculates about two possible endings to *Robinson Crusoe* and analyzes reasons for choosing or not choosing each of the two possible endings.

Think of two possible endings for the story Crusoe tells in his journal. Use the table below to organize your ideas. In the left column, write two possible endings. In the right column, give reasons why each ending could be possible. Base your reasons on evidence in the story. For example, think about what you know about Crusoe's personality or what you know or can infer about the island.

POSSIBLE ENDINGS	REASONS ENDINGS ARE POSSIBLE

GO

Sharing Your Plans With Others (Optional)

Before you begin writing, share your writing plans with some of your classmates. Using your notes, tell them about the two possible endings you have thought of. If you are not sure about two possible endings, tell your classmates about the ideas you are considering and get their reactions. Ask your classmates questions like the following:

- Would my possible endings be interesting to readers?
- Do my possible endings make sense based on the rest of the story?
- Is there anything else I should include in either ending or in the reasons that either ending is possible?

Jot down reactions from your classmates in the space below.

_____

_____

_____

_____

_____

_____

_____

_____

_____

_____

_____

_____

_____

_____

You should also be prepared to give comments and suggestions about your classmates' writing plans. Try to give them honest and specific suggestions. Tell them about things they may want to delete or add. Suggest ways they can organize their ideas.

GO ON

Thinking About Reactions

Spend a few minutes thinking about the comments and suggestions your classmates gave you. Review the notes you took when you met with them. Are there any changes you should make, based on their comments? Use the space below to write down any important ideas you received from your classmates or to revise your original writing plans.

_____

_____

_____

_____

_____

_____

_____

_____

_____

_____

_____

_____

_____

_____

_____

_____

_____

_____

_____

GO ON

Time to Write

Imagine that you are Daniel Defoe and are trying to finish your novel *Robinson Crusoe*. Write a letter to Jack Singleton, your friend and publisher, that does two things. Your letter should

1. speculate about two different possible endings to your story; and
2. discuss reasons for choosing or not choosing each of the two possible endings.

_____

_____

_____

_____

_____

_____

_____

_____

_____

_____

_____

_____

_____

_____

_____

_____

_____

_____

_____

_____

_____

_____

_____

ASSESSMENT • 3

LEVEL G

NAME _____

CLASS _____

DATE _____

**INTEGRATED
PERFORMANCE ASSESSMENT
STUDENT FORMS**

ASSESSMENT • 3

READING SECTION

➤ Directions:

Today you will read a poem and a journal entry. Then you will write about what you have read. You should write down your thoughts, questions, and opinions as you read. Your notes will help you when you write about the poem and journal entry. When you finish reading, answer all of the questions about the selections until you come to the word STOP.

Getting Ready to Read

William Wordsworth wrote the following poem, "I Wandered Lonely as a Cloud," in 1804. In his sister Dorothy Wordsworth's journal, an entry for Thursday, April 15th, 1802, describes the same field of daffodils that William Wordsworth so imaginatively renders in his verse.

Time to Read

As you read William Wordsworth's poem and Dorothy Wordsworth's journal entry, jot down notes about each writer's response to nature. What does each writer compare the flowers to?

I Wandered Lonely as a Cloud
by
William Wordsworth

> My thoughts about
> what I am reading

I wandered lonely as a cloud
    That floats on high o'er vales[1] and hills,
When all at once I saw a crowd,
    A host,[2] of golden daffodils,
Beside the lake, beneath the trees,
Fluttering and dancing in the breeze.

Continuous as the stars that shine
    And twinkle on the Milky Way,
They stretched in never-ending line
    Along the margin of a bay:[3]
Ten thousand saw I at a glance,
Tossing their heads in sprightly dance.

---

1. **vales:** wide valleys.
2. **host:** multitude.
3. **margin of a bay:** edge of the water.

GO ON

The waves beside them danced; but they
    Outdid the sparkling waves in glee:
A poet could not but be gay,
    In such jocund[4] company,
I gazed—and gazed—but little thought
What wealth the show to me had brought:

For oft, when on my couch I lie
    In vacant or in pensive mood,
They flash upon that inward eye
    Which is the bliss of solitude;
And then my heart with pleasure fills,
And dances with the daffodils.

> My thoughts about what I am reading

❦ ❦ ❦ ❦

from *The Journals*
by
Dorothy Wordsworth

Thursday, April 15th, 1802. It was a threatening misty morning—but mild. We set off after dinner from Eusemere. Mrs. Clarkson went a short way with us but turned back. The wind was furious and we thought we must have returned. We first rested in the large boathouse, then under a furze bush opposite Mr. Clarkson's. Saw the plow going in the field. The wind seized our breath the lake was rough. There was a boat by itself floating in the middle of the bay below Water Millock. We rested again in the Water Millock Lane. The hawthorns are black and green, the birches here and there greenish but there is yet more of purple to be seen on the twigs. We got over into a field to avoid some cows—people working, a few primroses by the roadside, woodsorrel flower, the anemone, scentless violets, strawberries, and that starry yellow flower which Mrs. C. calls pile wort. When we were in the woods beyond Gowbarrow Park we saw a few daffodils close to the water side. We fancied that the lake had floated the seeds ashore and that the little colony had so sprung up. But as we went along there were more and yet more and at last under the boughs of the trees, we saw that there was a long belt of them along the shore, about the breadth of a country turnpike road. I never saw daffodils so beautiful they grew among the mossy stones about and about them, some rested their heads upon these stones as on a pillow for weariness and the rest tossed and

---

4. **jocund:** cheerful, pleasant.

> GO ON

reeled and danced and seemed as if they verily laughed with the wind that blew upon them over the lake, they looked so gay ever glancing ever changing. This wind blew directly over the lake to them. There was here and there a little knot and a few stragglers a few yards higher up but they were so few as not to disturb the simplicity and unity and life of that one busy highway. . . .

My thoughts about what I am reading

GO ON

Responding to the Selection

Now that you have read the poem and journal entry, respond to the following items as completely as possible.

1. Take a few minutes to write down your first response to the poem and journal entry.

_____

_____

_____

_____

_____

_____

_____

_____

_____

_____

_____

_____

_____

_____

_____

_____

_____

_____

_____

| GO ON |

2. In the space below, sketch or describe images from these readings that are especially memorable or significant for you.

SKETCHES AND DESCRIPTIONS

Explain why you chose these images.

_____

_____

_____

_____

_____

_____

_____

_____

_____

GO ON

3. Think about the following quotations and complete the questions in the chart below.

QUOTATION FROM THE TEXT	LITERAL MEANING: WHAT IS THE WRITER SAYING?	PERSONAL RESPONSE: WHAT DO I THINK OF THE IDEA?	REFLECTIVE RESPONSE: WHAT DOES IT SAY ABOUT THE WORLD?
"I gazed—and gazed—but little thought/ What wealth the show to me had brought:"			
"...some rested their heads upon these stones as on a pillow for weariness and the rest tossed and reeled and danced and seemed as if they verily laughed with the wind that blew upon them over the lake, they looked so gay ever glancing ever changing."			

After you have filled in the chart, write one or two sentences explaining how you think William's and Dorothy's reflections on the flowers are different from each other.

_____

_____

_____

_____

GO ON

4. What do you think William Wordsworth means when he writes, "I wandered lonely as a cloud"? Why does he compare himself to a cloud?

_____

_____

_____

_____

_____

_____

_____

_____

_____

_____

_____

_____

_____

_____

_____

_____

_____

_____

_____

_____

_____

_____

_____

_____

GO ON

5. Create the first line of a poem in which you do what William Wordsworth does in the first line of his poem—compare a part of your life to something in nature. Then, explain why you chose that image from nature to say something about yourself.

_____

_____

_____

_____

_____

_____

_____

_____

_____

_____

_____

_____

_____

_____

_____

_____

_____

_____

_____

_____

_____

GO ON

6. Use this page to write down any additional thoughts you have about the poem and journal entry. Tell anything else about your understanding of the selections and what they mean to you.

_____

_____

_____

_____

_____

_____

_____

_____

_____

_____

_____

_____

_____

_____

_____

_____

_____

_____

_____

_____

_____

STOP!
DO NOT CONTINUE UNTIL INSTRUCTED
This is the end of the Reading Section

ASSESSMENT • 3
WRITING SECTION

Getting Ready to Write

You are going to write a reflective essay for your school newspaper. Your essay should discuss an ordinary experience or object that led you to have some new insight or insights about growing up. The purpose of your essay is to share your insights with your readers, not to convince them you are right.

What commonplace experience or object will you write about? What details will you include about the experience or object? What insights did you gain from this experience or object? Use the table below to organize your thoughts.

Ordinary experience or object I could write about:
Details about the experience or object:
Insights gained about growing up:

GO ON

Sharing Your Plans With Others (Optional)

Before you begin writing, share your writing plans with some of your classmates. Using your notes, tell them about the ordinary experiences or objects and the corresponding insights gained about growing up. If you are not sure which experience, object, or insights to write about, tell your classmates about the ideas you are considering and get their reactions. Ask your classmates questions like the following:

- If I have thought of more than one ordinary experience or object, which of them would be best to use for this writing assignment?

- Would my ordinary experience or object be familiar and interesting to readers?

- Is it clear how the insights I gained about growing up are related to the experience or object I am thinking of writing about?

Jot down reactions from your classmates in the space below.

_____

_____

_____

_____

_____

_____

_____

_____

_____

_____

_____

_____

_____

_____

You should also be prepared to give comments and suggestions about your classmates' writing plans. Try to give them honest and specific suggestions. Tell them about things they may want to delete or add. Suggest ways they can organize their ideas.

GO ON

Thinking About Reactions

Spend a few minutes thinking about the comments and suggestions your classmates gave you. Review the notes you took when you met with them. Are there any changes you should make, based on their comments? Use the space below to write down any important ideas you received from your classmates or to revise your original writing plans.

_____

_____

_____

_____

_____

_____

_____

_____

_____

_____

_____

_____

_____

_____

_____

_____

_____

_____

_____

_____

GO ON

Time to Write

You have been asked to write an essay for your school newspaper. The essay should have a philosophical tone—that is, it should describe a commonplace experience or object and then reflect about what that experience or object reveals about a particular aspect of growing up. You do not have to convince your readers that you are "right." You will simply be sharing your ideas and trying them out in an exploratory way. You may want to start by describing the everyday experience or ordinary object. Then explain what the experience or object reveals about growing up.

_____

_____

_____

_____

_____

_____

_____

_____

_____

_____

_____

_____

_____

_____

_____

_____

_____

_____

_____

_____

_____

_____

_____

_____

_____

_____

_____

_____

_____

_____

_____

_____

_____

_____

_____

_____

_____

_____

_____

_____

_____

_____

_____

_____

_____

_____

_____

_____

NAME _____

CLASS _____

DATE _____

INTEGRATED
PERFORMANCE ASSESSMENT
STUDENT FORMS

ASSESSMENT • 4

READING SECTION

➤ Directions:

Today you will read passages from an autobiography. Then you will write about what you have read. You should write down your thoughts, questions, and opinions as you read. Your notes will help you when you write about the reading selection. When you finish reading, answer all of the questions about the selection until you come to the word STOP.

Getting Ready to Read

The following reading selection is taken from *Testament of Youth*, an autobiography by English author Vera Brittain. In these passages, the author recounts some of her experiences in World War I. Brittain served as a nurse in a field hospital near the French village of Étaples, not far from the front lines of the war. At the time of the incidents described in the following passages, Brittain's fiancé had already been killed in battle and her brother Edward was fighting in Italy.

Time to Read

from *Testament of Youth*
by
Vera Brittain

> My thoughts about what I am reading

After days of continuous heavy duty and scamped, inadequate meals, our nerves were none too reliable, and I don't suppose I was the only member of the staff whose teeth chattered with sheer terror as we groped our way to our individual huts in response to the order to scatter. Hope Milroy and I, thinking that we might as well be killed together, sat glassy-eyed in her small, pitch-black room. Suddenly, intermittent flashes half blinded us, and we listened frantically in the deafening din for the bugle-call which we knew would summon us to join the night-staff in the wards if bombs began to fall on the hospital.

One young Sister,[1] who had previously been shelled at a Casualty Clearing Station, lost her nerve and rushed screaming through the Mess;[2] two others seized her and forcibly put her to bed, holding her down while the raid lasted to prevent her from causing a panic. I knew that I was more frightened than I had ever been in my life, yet all the time a tense, triumphant pride that I was not revealing my fear to the others held me to the semblance of self-control.

---

1. **Sister:** nurse.
2. **Mess:** a military dining hall or tent.

GO ON

When a momentary lull came in the booms and the flashes, Hope, who had also been under fire at a C.C.S., gave way to the sudden bravado of rushing into the open to see whether the raiders had gone; she was still wearing her white cap, and a dozen trembling hands instantly pulled her indoors again, a dozen shakily shrill voices scolded her indiscretion. Gradually, after another brief burst of firing, the camp became quiet, though the lights were not turned on again that night. Next day we were told that most of the bombs had fallen on the village; the bridge over the Canche, it was reported, had been smashed, and the train service had to be suspended while the engineers performed the exciting feat of mending it in twelve hours. . . .

Three weeks of such days and nights, lived without respite or off-duty time under the permanent fear of defeat and flight, reduced the staffs of the Étaples hospitals to the negative conviction that nothing mattered except to end the strain. England, panic-stricken, was frantically raising the military age to fifty and agreeing to the appointment of Foch[3] as Commander-in-Chief, but to us with our blistered feet, our swollen hands, our wakeful, reddened eyes, victory and defeat began—as indeed they were afterwards to prove—to seem very much the same thing. . . .

Early in April a letter arrived from my father to say that my mother had "crocked up" and had been obliged, owing to the inefficiency of the domestic help then available, to go into a nursing-home. What exactly was wrong remained unspecified, though phrases referred to "toxic heart" and "complete general breakdown." My father had temporarily closed the flat and moved into an hotel, but he did not, he told me, wish to remain there. "As your mother and I can no longer manage without you," he concluded, "it is now your duty to leave France immediately and return to Kensington."[4]

I read these words with real dismay, for my father's interpretation of my duty was not, I knew only too well, in the least likely to agree with that of the Army, which had always been singularly unmoved by the worries of relatives. What was I to do? I wondered desperately. There was my family, confidently demanding my presence, and here was the offensive, which made every pair of experienced hands worth ten pairs under normal conditions. . . .

Half-frantic with the misery of conflicting obligations, I envied Edward his complete powerlessness to leave the Army whatever happened at home. Today, remembering

> My thoughts about what I am reading

3. **Ferdinand Foch:** French marshall who in 1918 was appointed Commander-in-Chief of the Allied Forces (Britain, France, and the United States).
4. **Kensington:** a part of London.

GO ON

the violent clash between family and profession, between
"duty" and ambition, between conscience and achievement,
which has always harassed the women now in their thirties
and forties, I find myself still hoping that if the efforts of
various interested parties succeed in destroying the fragile
international structure built up since the Armistice, and war
breaks out on a scale comparable to that of 1914, the orga-
nizers of the machine will not hesitate to conscript all
women under fifty for service at home or abroad. In the long
run, an irrevocable allegiance in a time of emergency makes
decision easier for the older as well as for the younger gen-
eration. What exhausts women in wartime is not the strenu-
ous and unfamiliar tasks that fall upon them, nor even the
hourly dread of death for husbands or lovers or brothers or
sons; it is the incessant conflict between personal and
national claims which wears out their energy and breaks
their spirit.

That night, dizzy from work and indecision, I sat up in
bed listening for an air-raid and gazing stupidly at the flick-
ering shadows cast by the candle-lantern which was all the
illumination that we were now allowed. Through my brain
ran perpetually a short sentence which—having become,
like the men, liable to sudden light-headed intervals—I
could not immediately identify with anything that I had
read.

"'The strain all along,'" I repeated dully, "'is very
great . . . very great.'" What exactly did those words
describe? The enemy within shelling distance—refugee
Sisters crowding in with nerves all awry—bright moonlight,
and aeroplanes carrying machine-guns—ambulance trains
jolting noisily into the siding, all day, all night—gassed men
on stretchers, clawing the air—dying men, reeking with
mud and foul green-stained bandages, shrieking and
writhing in a grotesque travesty of manhood—dead men
with fixed, empty eyes and shiny, yellow faces. . . . Yes, perhaps the strain all along *had* been very great. . . .

Then I remembered; the phrase came out of my father's
letter, and it described, not the offensive in France, but the
troubles at home. The next day I went to the Matron's office
and interviewed the successor to the friendly Scottish
Matron who had sent me on leave, and whose health had
obliged her to leave Étaples and return to the calmer conditions of home service. The new Matron was old and charita-
ble, but she naturally did not welcome my problem with
enthusiasm. The application for long leave which I had
hoped to put in would have, she said, no chance at all while
this push was on; the only possibility was to break my contract, which I might be allowed to do if I made conditions at
home sound serious enough.

> My thoughts about
> what I am reading

Excerpt from *Testament of Youth* by Vera Brittain. Copyright 1933 by Vera Brittain. Reprinted by permission of **Paul Berry**, Literary Executor for Vera Brittain, and Virago Press, London.

GO ON

"I'm giving you this advice against my will," she added. "I'm already short of staff and I can't hope to replace you."

So, with a sinking heart, I asked for leave to break my contract owing to "special circumstances," and returned to my ward feeling a cowardly deserter. . . .

> My thoughts about
> what I am reading

Excerpt from *Testament of Youth* by Vera Brittain. Copyright 1933 by Vera Brittain. Reprinted by permission of **Paul Berry, Literary Executor for Vera Brittain, and Virago Press, London.**

GO ON

Responding to the Selection

Now that you have read the autobiographical passages, respond to the following items as completely as possible.

1. Take a few minutes to write down your first response to the autobiographical passages.

_____

_____

_____

_____

_____

_____

_____

_____

_____

_____

_____

_____

_____

_____

_____

_____

_____

_____

_____

_____

_____

_____

| GO ON |

2. In the box below, use words, pictures, or symbols to show how Brittain felt after she read her father's letter.

Now explain why you chose these words, pictures, or symbols.

_____

_____

_____

_____

_____

_____

_____

_____

_____

| GO ON |

3. In the space below, give your opinion of what Vera Brittain means by the following statement:

> What exhausts women in wartime is not the strenuous and unfamiliar tasks that fall upon them, nor even the hourly dread of death for husbands or lovers or brothers or sons; it is the incessant conflict between personal and national claims which wears out their energy and breaks their spirit.

_____

_____

_____

_____

_____

_____

_____

_____

_____

_____

_____

_____

_____

_____

_____

_____

_____

_____

_____

_____

GO ON

4. Brittain implies that the experience of serving one's country during war differs greatly between men and women. In the following chart, report your conclusions about how Brittain sees these differences. The chart also has a space for you to include your opinions about how men and women experience war.

	BRITTAIN'S THOUGHTS	MY THOUGHTS
Men in Wartime		
Women in Wartime		

5. Use this page to write down any additional thoughts you have about the autobiographical passages. Tell anything else about your understanding of the passages and
what they mean to you.

_____

_____

_____

_____

_____

_____

_____

_____

_____

_____

_____

_____

_____

_____

_____

_____

_____

_____

_____

STOP!
DO NOT CONTINUE UNTIL INSTRUCTED
This is the end of the Reading Section

ASSESSMENT • 4
WRITING SECTION

Getting Ready to Write

At some point in their lives, many people feel torn between two conflicting obligations—duty to school versus duty to work, duty to community versus duty to self, duty to classes versus duty to clubs or sports teams. You will focus on a conflict of this kind and write a report of information for your social science teacher about the experience of having conflicting obligations. You will not take sides in the conflict. Instead, you will concentrate on clearly describing the nature of the conflict.

Think about people—real or fictional—who have had to choose between two conflicting duties. They may be people you know or people you have read about or seen on TV or in movies. What conflicting obligations did they face? What examples could you provide to illustrate the conflict? Use the chart below to list some of your ideas before you begin writing.

People with conflicting obligations:
Examples of their conflicting obligations:
Explanation of why the choices were difficult for the people to make:

GO ON

Sharing Your Plans With Others (Optional)

Before you begin writing, share your writing plans with some of your classmates. Using your notes, tell them about the conflicting obligations you plan to write about and what you will say about them. If you are not sure which conflicting obligations to write about, tell your classmates about the conflicting obligations you are considering and get their reactions. Ask your classmates questions like the following:

- Have I chosen a pair of conflicting obligations that will be interesting to others?

- Am I taking an objective view of the problem?

- Have I overlooked anything important I should include about the conflicting obligations?

Jot down reactions from your classmates in the space below.

_____

_____

_____

_____

_____

_____

_____

_____

_____

_____

_____

_____

_____

_____

_____

_____

You should also be prepared to give comments and suggestions about your classmates' writing plans. Try to give them honest and specific suggestions. Tell them about things they may want to delete or add. Suggest ways they can organize their ideas.

GO ON

Thinking About Reactions

Spend a few minutes thinking about the comments and suggestions your classmates gave you. Review the notes you took when you met with them. Are there any changes you should make, based on their comments? Use the space below to write down any important ideas you received from your classmates or to revise your original writing plans.

_____

_____

_____

_____

_____

_____

_____

_____

_____

_____

_____

_____

_____

_____

_____

_____

_____

_____

_____

_____

_____

_____

_____

Time to Write

Write a report of information for your social science teacher in which you describe a conflict of obligations that people have experienced. In your report, do not take sides in the conflict. Instead, concentrate on clearly describing the nature of the conflict you have chosen to write about. Include examples from personal experience, from news reports you have seen or read, or from the lives of fictional characters in books, TV, or films. Present an objective report on the problem and try to make your report informative and engaging.

_____

_____

_____

_____

_____

_____

_____

_____

_____

_____

_____

_____

_____

_____

_____

_____

_____

_____

_____

_____

_____

_____

COPYING MASTERS OF CHECKLISTS

Reading/Writing Observational Checklist, Part 1 96

Reading/Writing Observational Checklist, Part 2 97

Speaking/Listening Observational Checklist...98

Teacher _____

Assessment _____

Setting of the Observation _____

Date _____

Class _____

Part 1: Observing the Reading Process

Using Effective Strategies																
Sets own purpose for reading																
Makes connections between the text and prior knowledge and experience																
Anticipates and predicts what the author might say																
Thinks about words or phrases to stay focused on meaning																
Rereads if things don't make sense																
Seeks help from teacher or peers when necessary for understanding																
Takes marginal notes or draws diagrams to aid comprehension																

Student Names

Marking Key
+ Consistently
o Occasionally
— Never

Level G

TEACHER _____ DATE _____

ASSESSMENT _____ CLASS _____

PART 2: OBSERVING THE WRITING PROCESS

SETTING OF THE OBSERVATION _____

PLANNING															
Uses prewriting strategies															
Develops a plan before writing															
Applies prewriting plans															
Rewriting															
Shows awareness of purpose and audience															
Makes word-level revisions (e.g., spelling, punctuation, word changes															
Makes higher-level revisions (e.g., adding ideas, removing parts, moving sentences or paragraphs)															
Self-evaluating															
Seeks reactions from others															
Evaluates and uses the reactions of others															
Reflects on quality of own work															

STUDENT NAMES

MARKING KEY	
+	Consistently
o	Occasionally
—	Never

SPEAKING/LISTENING OBSERVATIONAL CHECKLIST

STUDENT NAMES

SPEAKING

Volunteers for speaking activities													
Makes comments that are appropriate to the situation													
Expresses ideas clearly and accurately													
Presents ideas in an organized manner													
Supports point of view with logical evidence													
Responds logically to comments of others													
Rephrases or adjusts if others don't understand													

LISTENING

Attends to what others are saying													
Exhibits reactions (e.g., facial expressions) that reflect comprehension													
Understands directions without needing repetition													
Ignores distractions													

MARKING KEY

+	Consistently
o	Occasionally
—	Never

MODEL PAPERS WITH ANNOTATIONS

Assessment 1 ....**101**

READING: Poem
    High 102
    Medium 108
    Low 114

WRITING: Autobiographical Incident (Narrative)
    High 120
    Medium 123
    Low 125

Assessment 2 ....**127**

READING: Novel, excerpt
    High 128
    Medium 133
    Low 138

WRITING: Speculation about Causes and Effects (Expository)
    High 143
    Medium 145
    Low 147

Assessment 3 ....**149**

READING: Poem/Journal, excerpt
    High 150
    Medium 156
    Low 162

WRITING: Reflective Essay (Expository)
    High 168
    Medium 171
    Low 174

Assessment 4 ....**175**

READING: Autobiography, excerpt
    High 176
    Medium 181
    Low 186

WRITING: Informative Report (Expository)
    High 191
    Medium 194
    Low 196

ASSESSMENT • 1

READING: POEM
WRITING: AUTOBIOGRAPHICAL INCIDENT
(NARRATIVE)

Responding to the Selection

Now that you have read the poem, respond to the following items as completely as possible.

1. Take a few minutes to write down your first response to the poem.

The Wanderer is a lyric telling of a warriors
depression in the aftermath of a raid
in which all but himself have died.
He is alone and cannot find any comfort
in his stark surroundings. He wonders
about his current situation while
lamenting about the glorious days of
the past when he had everything.
The warrior keeps going back to the past
and imagining the kinsmen and his
lord but must return to reality to
find nothing there. He feels guilty
about being the only one left alive.
He travels in the hopes to find a life
like the life in his past before the raid,
but fails to find it. In anger the
warrior talks of the corruption of the
world that killed off everything he
lived for. Towards the end of the lyric
the warrior understands that he must
look to God, the only one who he can seek
help from, who is not of the evil world,

response continues

2. As the speaker in the poem "cuts" aimlessly through the frozen seas in search of a welcoming port, he says that "Fate" offers him only one comfort—that of "memory." In the chart below, compare some of the feelings and experiences the Wanderer has as an exile to those he relives from the past.

	THE WANDERER'S PRESENT	THE WANDERER'S PAST
A	loneliness endless roaming to find something to live for	always around people of his kind. part of a crowd with same goals.
B	no one knows the worrier or tries to comfort him with feasts.	The men all knew each other well, always had fun (in feasts) comfortable around his friends.
C	he longs for his lord, he feels unloved without him, and very alone	he worshipped his lord, who was ruler. The warrior loved him, placed him on a pedestal.
D	Kinsmen: "The best of friends" welcomed and greeted fondly ←→ Switch!	only faded memories, silence instead of friendly chatter nothing.
E	men were robbed of their wealth, looted & killed.	men were wealthy
F	wrecks, a coffin for those who died in it.	proud warriors, great buildings

response continues

3. How are the speaker's emotions reflected in the poem's physical setting? List at least four details of the setting and explain how they mirror the Wanderer's feelings.

	SETTING DESCRIPTION	HOW IT REFLECTS THE WANDERER'S FEELINGS
A	Frost cold foam of sea	his heart is cold and feels nothing
B	lonely dawns "grey with mourning"	a sadness in a setting that is supposed to be serene
C	"weary winter" frozen waves	he is weary of roaming around trying to find a new life. He is at a stagnant time in life.
D	"rocky slopes are beaten by storms, / This earth pinned down by driving snow"	He feels ~~too~~ defeated and cannot see any reason to go on
E		
F		

response continues

4. Until it was written down by a Christian monk, "The Wanderer" was sung from memory rather than read from a page. Like *Beowulf*, "The Wanderer" is an oral elegy that harpist-bards performed for audiences in communal gathering places like the "mead–halls" mentioned in the poem.

   Imagine how the poem sounded back in A.D. 940 when sung by a bard accompanied on a harp. Then stretch your imagination a little further and describe a modern-day song which reminds you of "The Wanderer." As you describe the modern-day song, explain how it is similar to and/or different from the poem. Why does the song remind you of this poem?

"The Wanderer" is reminiscent of Michael Card's "Job Suite" which is a song adapted from the Bible. Job was a rich man who was very blessed, but in one holocaust, all his riches were gone and his family killed. He did have reason to sulk around and be depressed, but he was a firm believer in God. Job looked to God during this time of troubles. The men that Job came in contact with did not welcome Job because he believed in God and they did not. So Job is alone, with God as his only hope. Job professes the power of God and tells him he has nothing more to say than this.

The warrior in "The Wanderer" loses everything also, and has nothing to speak for. He, like Job, looks to God, who is the only stronghold in a world filled with so much evil.

response continues

5. Read the first two lines and the last verse (lines 111–115) of the poem. Some critics have argued that the first two lines and the last verse of "The Wanderer" were added by the Christian monk who preserved the poem in writing. Do you agree? Using specific evidence from the poem to back up your opinion, explain why you do or do not agree with these critics' argument.

The Christian monk who preserved the poem may have added these lines about God to give the poem a moral. Since the monk is one who is a devout follower of God, this may have happened. The poem without the lines about God gives no evidence of believing or blaming God. Also, the first and last lines are in third person, while the rest of the poem is a cry from the warrior in first person.

response continues

6. Use this page to write down any additional thoughts you have about the poem. Tell anything else about your understanding of the poem and what it means to you.

The Wanderer is expresses his lament and longing for his previous life. This is similar to how people often look back to a time in their life when they were content, even if they didn't realize how many things they had to be grateful for at the time, upon reflection, they are able to see the joyful experiences they may no longer have. Others remember things better than they may have been. But everyone experiences losses of some kind or another — the Wanderer's losses seem profound.

Annotation for HIGH Reading Model • Score 6

This paper represents a thoughtful and perceptive interpretation of the poem. Unlike the writers of papers at lower score points, this student continually searches for meaning that goes beyond a literal interpretation. For example, the responses to Item 3 are sophisticated and display an ability to interpret symbolism. The response to Item 4 weakens the overall paper slightly because the student does not fully and logically develop the connection between "The Wanderer" and a modern-day song. However, the response to Item 6 displays the student's ability to extend the poem by reflecting on its universal implications. Overall, the response is exemplary and demonstrates excellent comprehension.

Responding to the Selection

Now that you have read the poem, respond to the following items as completely as possible.

1. Take a few minutes to write down your first response to the poem.

This man was exiled from his clan. He is
lonely and longs to be with his lord. Everything he has known is gone. I
    In the end of the passage, it
seems the man gained wisdom about
life.
    Guard your faith, don't let your
grief show.

response continues

2. As the speaker in the poem "cuts" aimlessly through the frozen seas in search of a welcoming port, he says that "Fate" offers him only one comfort—that of "memory." In the chart below, compare some of the feelings and experiences the Wanderer has as an exile to those he relives from the past.

	THE WANDERER'S PRESENT	THE WANDERER'S PAST
A	They are dead.	He remembers his friends.
B	Alas he is alone.	He remembers joy in his Lord's presence.
C	Everthing is destroyed	The happy days full of feasting and happiness.
D	The whole scene around him is empty.	War has destroyed everything he has ever known.
E	The Wanderer has no more warmth.	Happy times the Wanderer had with his lord
F	Sees Wreckage	Remembers a dark twisted life full of endless slaughters.

response continues

3. How are the speaker's emotions reflected in the poem's physical setting? List at least four details of the setting and explain how they mirror the Wanderer's feelings.

	SETTING DESCRIPTION	HOW IT REFLECTS THE WANDERER'S FEELINGS
A	On frozen waves, hoping to find a place, a people, a lord to replace my lost ones	The wanderer still does not realize he is alone
B	Watch the frost the snow and the hail.	He longs for his lord.
C	The wreckage (ruins)	He feels that he was once happy like the buildings, but now he is alone and depleted like the ruins.
D		
E		
F		

response continues

4. Until it was written down by a Christian monk, "The Wanderer" was sung from memory rather than read from a page. Like *Beowulf*, "The Wanderer" is an oral elegy that harpist-bards performed for audiences in communal gathering places like the "mead–halls" mentioned in the poem.

Imagine how the poem sounded back in A.D. 940 when sung by a bard accompanied on a harp. Then stretch your imagination a little further and describe a modern-day song which reminds you of "The Wanderer." As you describe the modern-day song, explain how it is similar to and/or different from the poem. Why does the song remind you of this poem?

I can't think of a song this poem would remind me of. I can describe a song that would correspond to "The Wanderer."

The song would be slow and steady. The words would be full of emotion and meaning. The words would be heard over the music.

response continues

5. Read the first two lines and the last verse (lines 111–115) of the poem. Some critics have argued that the first two lines and the last verse of "The Wanderer" were added by the Christian monk who preserved the poem in writing. Do you agree? Using specific evidence from the poem to back up your opinion, explain why you do or do not agree with these critics' argument.

    I do think the monk added the lines Because the Wanderer was totally devoted to his lord, not God. The monk felt the poem needed something to glorify God. The Wanderer doesn't seem to think of God anywhere else in the story other than the beginning and ending.

    The Wanderer also seems to have hope in the beginning and end. In the middle he doesn't. This leads me to believe that the Christian Monk added them to the poem.

response continues

6. Use this page to write down any additional thoughts you have about the poem. Tell anything else about your understanding of the poem and what it means to you.

The man is suffering through a lot. He is alone. He just has memories of his past to keep him happy and focused. I think he needs to "wake-up" and find something to live for.

Annotation for MEDIUM Reading Model • Score 3

This student displays a literal and simplistic understanding of the text. The response opens with a very brief plot summary (see Item 1). The comparisons made in Item 2 are rather superficial and not always parallel. Also, some of the connections made in Item 3 between setting descriptions and the Wanderer's feelings are not logical. In Item 4 the student compares the poem to a "slow and steady" song but does not explain this assessment. The answer to Item 5 is relatively stronger than responses to other items, but the response to Item 6 is very superficial. Overall, this student demonstrates only a limited understanding of the poem and exhibits little reflective thinking.

Responding to the Selection

Now that you have read the poem, respond to the following items as completely as possible.

1. Take a few minutes to write down your first response to the poem.

At first it was kinda confusing to me in some points. I thought things that were probebly way off the to what the poet was trying to say but then some things I think I kinda got a grip on what was being said and why. But mainly in the begining it was confusing besides I usually don't understand poems anyways they always have and probebly always will confuse me.

response continues

2. As the speaker in the poem "cuts" aimlessly through the frozen seas in search of a welcoming port, he says that "Fate" offers him only one comfort—that of "memory." In the chart below, compare some of the feelings and experiences the Wanderer has as an exile to those he relives from the past. *I don't understand*

	THE WANDERER'S PRESENT	THE WANDERER'S PAST
A		
B		
C		
D		
E		
F		

response continues

3. How are the speaker's emotions reflected in the poem's physical setting? List at least four details of the setting and explain how they mirror the Wanderer's feelings.

	SETTING DESCRIPTION	HOW IT REFLECTS THE WANDERER'S FEELINGS
A	Sadness has never driven sadness off.	he's sad and upset
B	Without deepest dreams of losing	he's thinking of how it is + what it means
C	The warmth is dead	he's hurt & feels lonely
D	Because I never 4-got the faith	he's remembering and I think he's kinda sad but a little happy
E	And deeply considers this dark twisted life	I think he was wishing he was dead
F		

response continues

4. Until it was written down by a Christian monk, "The Wanderer" was sung from memory rather than read from a page. Like *Beowulf*, "The Wanderer" is an oral elegy that harpist-bards performed for audiences in communal gathering places like the "mead–halls" mentioned in the poem.

   Imagine how the poem sounded back in A.D. 940 when sung by a bard accompanied on a harp. Then stretch your imagination a little further and describe a modern-day song which reminds you of "The Wanderer." As you describe the modern-day song, explain how it is similar to and/or different from the poem. Why does the song remind you of this poem?

The Wanderer doesn't really remind me of any song or anything so I couldn't really compare it with anything

response continues

5. Read the first two lines and the last verse (lines 111–115) of the poem. Some critics have argued that the first two lines and the last verse of "The Wanderer" were added by the Christian monk who preserved the poem in writing. Do you agree? Using specific evidence from the poem to back up your opinion, explain why you do or do not agree with these critics' argument.

I don't understand what I supposed to agree or disagree with

response continues

6. Use this page to write down any additional thoughts you have about the poem. Tell anything else about your understanding of the poem and what it means to you.

This poem was very confusing and at parts I thought I understood but I really didn't. I can't stand poems so I really didn't like this. The poem kinda means to me that people are always looking for somewhere to go and not knowing what they should do with themselfs to to find where they should go. But the poem did have a lot of really neat and pretty lines in it even though I didn't understand them, they sounded nice.

Annotation for LOW Reading Model • Score 1

This response reflects the student's frustration and confusion in attempting to comprehend the poem. In various responses, the student expresses his or her inability to make meaning of the selection or understand questions about the text (e.g., "…it was kinda confusing…": Item 1; "I don't understand what I supposed to agree or disagree with": Item 5). This lack of comprehension is also evident in Item 4 as the student is unable to make associations between the poem and any modern-day songs.

Time to Write

Assume that you are writing a letter to a friend you have not seen for some time. In your letter, relate an incident you have experienced that improved your outlook of yourself, someone else, or the world. Remember that an "incident" occurs within a short span of time—a few minutes, a few hours, or a day.

Be sure to give your autobiographical incident a beginning, middle, and end. Provide specific details (including descriptions of how things looked, felt, sounded, tasted, and smelled) that will help your friend imagine the incident and how you felt as you had the experience. After reading the letter, your friend should understand why the incident was important to you.

Dear Carol,

Hi! How have you been? I'm doing just great down here. Well, you wouldn't believe what happened a few weeks ago! Lenny actually came to me for help! Yes, this is the same Lenny, my older brother, who rarely speaks to me unless he wants something. I couldn't believe it! I was sitting in bed while on the phone with Jill. I was in my pyjamas and all toasty warm, when I hear a quiet knock at my door. Lenny said, "Fran, you in there? Are you dressed?" I replied that I was changed, and told him to get lost like I usually do. He did. A few minutes later he comes to the door again, "Fran? come here I've got to talk to you." I couldn't believe what I was seeing and hearing. Picture Lenny at my door with a tear in his eye at my door, asking me for help. Me, of all people! Well, I quickly got off the phone with Jill, changed clothes, and went to go talk to Lenny.

response continues

As I walked down the stairs to the foyer, my heart was racing. For him to come to me, I figured it was something he was afraid to tell our parents. This got me worried. A thousand thoughts went through my mind in that span of about seven seconds. I thought "Oh my God! He's got to have some awful disease. Hopefully, it's something a little less drastic, like maybe he got into a car accident, or he was in a fight with someone.

As I walked out onto our driveway, where he was waiting, a chill came over me. It was about 9:30 or 10:00 PM and there were many stars shining above. Lenny was pacing the driveway. I said, "Lenny? Are you o.k.? What happened?" He ran over to me and just kept hugging me as he cried. He was so distrought, that he couldn't even speak straight, so I decided to ask him yes and no questions so he would only have to nod. I asked if he was hurt—no. I asked if someone else was hurt—no. He took a while and said, "I got dumped on my ... again." I said "Nadine dumped you?" He nodded yes and a sense of relief came over me. I never liked her

response continues

Annotation for HIGH Writing Model • Rhetorical Effectiveness: Score 5
The writer of this response presents a coherent, engaging, and well-developed account of a specific incident. Although the incident itself is not extremely remarkable, the writer has elevated its significance by skillfully building suspense through the use of sensory details, dialogue, and internal monologue. The response displays strong personal involvement and an authentic voice that make a somewhat ordinary incident seem especially important.

(annotation continues on next page)

and I was glad she was out of his life. I was also happy that it wasn't anything worse. I also felt bad for him because he was hurting

We stayed outside and talked for a half hour in the cold. I told him that if he ever needs me, he can come to me and I'll be there for him. I couldn't believe that he opened up to me like that. He actually showed his soft, vulnerable side to his own sister! Ever since then, he's been nicer and more open to me. I respect him so much for coming to me and letting his feelings show.

So, how are things with you? You have to send me a letter with a picture of you in it. Every one here misses you. I'll talk to you soon!

Love,

Fran

Annotation for HIGH Writing Model • Conventions: Score 5
The response demonstrates successful use of the conventions of written language. A few minor mechanics and spelling errors prevent the paper from earning a score of 6.

Time to Write

Assume that you are writing a letter to a friend you have not seen for some time. In your letter, relate an incident you have experienced that improved your outlook of yourself, someone else, or the world. Remember that an "incident" occurs within a short span of time—a few minutes, a few hours, or a day.

Be sure to give your autobiographical incident a beginning, middle, and end. Provide specific details (including descriptions of how things looked, felt, sounded, tasted, and smelled) that will help your friend imagine the incident and how you felt as you had the experience. After reading the letter, your friend should understand why the incident was important to you.

> Three weeks ago we lost to St. Charles, I cried like a baby. It wasn't because we lost, I can handle that, it's just that I would never play football again. I didn't take my helmet off for a least an hour after the game was over, for fear it would be my last time. I never knew How much I loved the game till I realized it was over. Last Thursday was our awards night + Mr. Thorne had some nice things to say about me, but what sticks out most was when he said "There may be a Minor league football team at Penn State." My mind wandered as I saw Images of me suiting up again. We'll have to wait + see, my dreams of playing college football at Penn STATE may come True

Annotation for MEDIUM Writing Model • Rhetorical Effectiveness: Score 3

In this response the writer relates a specific incident but does not develop it adequately. The student also does a sketchy job of establishing the context. The reader must infer that the writer is a senior playing in his last high school football game. The reader also must interpret the importance of the incident. The student's main point is probably embedded in one sentence (i.e., "I never knew How much I loved the game till I realized it was over"). Although there is evidence of personal involvement, the lack of elaboration, orientation, and an explicit statement of the incident's significance cause this response to receive a score of 3.

(annotation continues on next page)

Annotation for MEDIUM Writing Model • Conventions: Score 3
The response also receives a score of 3 in Conventions. The paper is coherent, but a few usage errors and numerous errors in mechanics are evident.

Time to Write

Assume that you are writing a letter to a friend you have not seen for some time. In your letter, relate an incident you have experienced that improved your outlook of yourself, someone else, or the world. Remember that an "incident" occurs within a short span of time—a few minutes, a few hours, or a day.

Be sure to give your autobiographical incident a beginning, middle, and end. Provide specific details (including descriptions of how things looked, felt, sounded, tasted, and smelled) that will help your friend imagine the incident and how you felt as you had the experience. After reading the letter, your friend should understand why the incident was important to you.

Dear Rebecca

Hey Girl? Its been a long time since I've seen you. When are you coming down to see me again? I hope soon! Well, a lot has happened since you left, I met someone new. He is great! His name is Jason. I can't wait till you met him!

Jason is so much different than Sammy, and we have so much fun together. I think we're going to last. Sammy still talks to me — let me tell you what happened just yesterday — He Sat by me in 5th period. I could not believe it. I truely liked to have almost fell over.

Like I said, you are just going to have to come see me soon girl! We'll got a lot to share!

Please Write Back as soon as possible and tell me everything that is happening in

response continues

Annotation for LOW Writing Model • Rhetorical Effectiveness: Score 1

In this response the writer tells her friend about meeting "someone new." Although the response exhibits some evidence of personal involvement, a glaring lack of development and elaboration is also apparent. In addition, details and dialogue are missing, and very little context is provided. Instead, the writer relies on trite generalizations (". . . we have so much fun together. I think we're going to last"). The writer does refer very briefly and vaguely to an incident ("He sat by me in 5th period"), but it is unclear to whom she is referring or the significance of the incident.

(annotation concludes on next page)

your life right now.
Love Ya,
Alyssa

Annotation for LOW Writing Model • Conventions: Score 3
The response demonstrates marginally successful use of the conventions of written language. Several minor errors in mechanics, usage, and spelling are evident, but the errors do not seriously disrupt the meaning of the response.

ASSESSMENT • 2

READING: NOVEL, EXCERPT
WRITING: SPECULATION ABOUT CAUSES AND EFFECTS (EXPOSITORY)

Responding to the Selection

Now that you have read the novel passages, respond to the following items as completely as possible.

1. Take a few minutes to write down your first response to the passages.

It seems to me that Carlso is trying to come to terms with his personal situation. He is suffering from great fear and anxiety and because he views these feelings to be irrational, he makes every attempt to calm his mind. To me, this is quite admirable. I have always felt that logic should rule over emotions, and, thus far, I am quite impressed.

The other thing I noticed about these journal entries is that they are not entries written impromptu. He has given great thought to every single entry and has arrived at personal conclusions. These entries are not a personal outreach, but rather a written record of his own conclusions.

response continues

2. Why do you think Crusoe starts and keeps writing in his journal?

I believe Crusoe starts his journal and keeps writing in it because he needs a form of human interaction. Often, people share their feelings and experiences with other people. Crusoe, being the only person on the island, is forced to turn to himself. However, instead of having a conversation with a mirror, he takes to writing.

Crusoe also takes to writing to comfort himself. If people keep all of their feelings bottled up inside of them, they have great inner turmoil. Crusoe felt his need to express himself, and writing seemed to be his only reasonable outlet.

response continues

3. After he is shipwrecked, Crusoe makes a list of the evil and good aspects of his situation. He concludes that "there was scarce any condition in the world so miserable, but there was something negative or something positive to be thankful for in it." Do you agree or disagree with his conclusion? Explain the reasons for your opinion.

I agree with Crusoe's statement that "there [is] scarce any condition in the world so miserable but that there was something positive to be thankful for in it." The reason why I agree with this statement is that even in the most miserable conditions, it is impossible to go on unless you can see a positive aspect. Whenever anything goes wrong, there is always the possibility that things could have gone worse. That realization in and of itself adds a positive glimmer to any negative situation.

response continues

4. What three adjectives do you think best describe Crusoe? In the chart below, list the adjectives and then give reasons for your choices.

ADJECTIVE THAT DESCRIBES CRUSOE	REASONS THAT IT DESCRIBES CRUSOE
Logical	He wrote out a chart to work through his emotions. He recognises harmful attitudes & does his best to put them a side. He made every attempt to organize his home.
RESOURCEFUL	He went to the shipwreck & scavenged all that he possibly could. He used the leaves to protect him from the rain. He learned how to make planks & build.
OPTIMISTIC	Robin wrote a list of pros & cons. He always gave more creedence to the positive facets.

response continues

5. Use this page to write down any additional thoughts you have about the passages. Tell anything else about your understanding of the selection and what it means to you.

Now that I have been introduced to this novel, and had a chance to admire Caruso's logic, resourcefulness, and optimistic outlook I might look for the book in the library. I would like to read more about his adventures and find out how Defoe really ended the story.

Annotation for HIGH Reading Model • Score 6
This student exhibits a perceptive and insightful understanding of the passages. Unlike so many students who give a simple plot summary in response to Item 1, this student leaps immediately to an analysis of the character's motive and draws connections between the character's behavior and his or her understanding of human nature. The adjectives the reader uses to describe Crusoe (see Item 4) are appropriate and well supported with evidence from the story. The response to Item 5 demonstrates personal engagement and an appreciation of the literature selection.

Responding to the Selection

Now that you have read the novel passages, respond to the following items as completely as possible.

1. Take a few minutes to write down your first response to the passages.

This book is not something I'd choose for myself to read. But after going through just these few passages I find myself curious as to how Crusoe fares after he finds the footprint.

Are there really people there after so many years? If there are, will Robinson be willing to return to what is probably an existance in society & civilization that he's totally unprepared for.

How does he look? Is he still recognizable as a man?

response continues

2. **Why do you think Crusoe starts and keeps writing in his journal?**

Crusoe started & kept a journal
because he'd go insane otherwise.
The journal took on the
form of human companionship
for Crusoe. No matter that it
couldn't respond, or conversate. It
also couldn't insult or reject.
Maybe he kept the journal
to keep his hope of being
rescued alive.

response continues

3. After he is shipwrecked, Crusoe makes a list of the evil and good aspects of his situation. He concludes that "there was scarce any condition in the world so miserable, but there was something negative or something positive to be thankful for in it." Do you agree or disagree with his conclusion? Explain the reasons for your opinion.

If I had the same human qualities as Crusoe, I'd probably agree & appreciate what he says

But I dont really agree with it because I'd be wishing I were one of the ones sunk to the bottom of the ocean. The reason for this being that one of my greatest fears is to be absolutely alone in the world.

response continues

4. **What three adjectives do you think best describe Crusoe? In the chart below, list the adjectives and then give reasons for your choices.**

ADJECTIVE THAT DESCRIBES CRUSOE	REASONS THAT IT DESCRIBES CRUSOE
Resourceful	he lives on ~~are~~ a deserted island for years upon years w/o civilization nearby. Wouldn't you call that resourceful.
Strong- -minded & -willed	he manages not to go insane w/o ~~s~~ any contact besides that of the animals.
resigned	he gives up hope that ships are coming for him & decides to make a life, if you could call it that, for himself on the island.

response continues

5. Use this page to write down any additional thoughts you have about the passages. Tell anything else about your understanding of the selection and what it means to you.

I understand ~~what~~ what the books means & I am really curious as to how the story turns out as I've had more real interest in the story before & didn't pay attention when it was mentioned in my presence.

Maybe I'll go buy a copy.

Annotation for MEDIUM Reading Model • Score 4
This response represents a thoughtful reading performance. Although much of the interpretation is at the literal level, the student does seem to be engaged with the text. For example, note the questions the reader raises in her or his own mind in response to Item 1 and the curiosity about the novel expressed in Item 5. Also, the character analysis revealed in Item 4 displays a thoughtful interpretation. The response to Item 3 shows that the student makes meaningful associations between Crusoe's experiences and his or her own. On balance, this paper has enough strengths to merit a score of 4.

Responding to the Selection

Now that you have read the novel passages, respond to the following items as completely as possible.

1. Take a few minutes to write down your first response to the passages.

It is a very interesting reading. But if I was Crusoe I would go on a hunt or a search party by him self. I would be looking for the person hows footprint I found. I would grab my gun and ax instead of Staying in his little house been worried and scared.

response continues

2. Why do you think Crusoe starts and keeps writing in his journal?

I think Crusoe starts a journal to keep track of what he did. If he gets rescued he has something he can look back on.

response continues

3. After he is shipwrecked, Crusoe makes a list of the evil and good aspects of his situation. He concludes that "there was scarce any condition in the world so miserable, but there was something negative or something positive to be thankful for in it." Do you agree or disagree with his conclusion? Explain the reasons for your opinion.

I agree there is something to be grateful for. He should be greatfull, he is still alive. The dead people's lives are over. He can still go on and finish his life. Maybe do something with his life.

response continues

4. What three adjectives do you think best describe Crusoe? In the chart below, list the adjectives and then give reasons for your choices.

ADJECTIVE THAT DESCRIBES CRUSOE	REASONS THAT IT DESCRIBES CRUSOE
Inteligent	He stops and thinks about the sutitation his in. He descides to make a fort or home for himself and he keeps a journal.
Survivor	He makes his home. Goes to the ship wreck get a gun a ax and other useful things. for his survival
human.	He is human so he has fear. He is not perfect. And he wouldint tolerate those cats.

response continues

5. Use this page to write down any additional thoughts you have about the passages. Tell anything else about your understanding of the selection and what it means to you.

I think it is a good story but it is just not interesting enough for me. I think you should make it more interesting, such as put a woman in to the story.

Annotation for LOW Reading Model • Score 2

This student exhibits limited reading performance. Although the responses are stronger than those usually found in score 1 papers, they are still rather superficial. The student does make personal, though limited, connections in the initial reaction (see Item 1). In Item 2, the suggested reason why Crusoe kept a journal ("... to keep track of what he did") is plausible but much less insightful than responses seen in higher-scoring papers. The response to Item 4 is a stronger part of this paper and is characteristic of papers receiving scores of 3 or 4. However, when all responses are viewed holistically, the paper does not have enough strengths to earn a score higher than 2.

Time to Write

Imagine that you are Daniel Defoe and are trying to finish your novel *Robinson Crusoe*. Write a letter to Jack Singleton, your friend and publisher, that does two things. Your letter should

1. speculate about two different possible endings to your story; and
2. discuss reasons for choosing or not choosing each of the two possible endings.

Dear Jack,

As you know by now I'm well on my way to finishing my new novel *Robinson Crusoe*. A lot of time, energy and thought has gone into my new project and now I am faced with a dilemma - How am I ever going to wrap this one up?

From the start I'd always figured I'd have Robinson Crusoe live. He'd have his adventure on the island and then somehow a someway be rescued. It's all set to have an ending like that. In the last chapter I wrote in an extra set of footprints and I can have him rescued but now I'm having second thoughts.

Do you think his death would appeal to readers. Books can sometimes be very dull and predictable so what if I have these footprints belong to an unfriendly vistor who does away with Mr. Crusoe?

response continues

Annotation for HIGH Writing Model • Rhetorical Effectiveness: Score 6

The introductory paragraph of this response convinces the reader that this really could be a letter from the author to his publisher. Building on the publisher's awareness of the situation, the writer speculates about two possible endings, using logical and inventive reasons to argue confidently for "the latter of the two." The writer provides multiple perspectives and excellent insights ("Books can sometimes be very dull and predictable . . . So much emphasis has gone into writting this character with a positive attitude, so what if I surprise my audience with a tragic ending?").

(annotation continues on next page)

So much emphasis has gone into writing this character with a positive attitude, so what if I surprise my audience with a tragic ending?

I think I could sell it. Jack if you let me do the latter of the two endings I think this book will be a hit! Give me the chance, see what you think. It doesn't have to be permanent. Any advice you can give me would be greatly appreciated. You know I trust your opinion. I'll be hearing from you soon.

Sincerely —
Daniel Defoe

Annotation for HIGH Writing Model • Conventions: Score 5
This student demonstrates successful use of the conventions of written language. Several minor errors in usage and mechanics prevent this paper from receiving a score of 6.

Time to Write

Imagine that you are Daniel Defoe and are trying to finish your novel *Robinson Crusoe*. Write a letter to Jack Singleton, your friend and publisher, that does two things. Your letter should

1. speculate about two different possible endings to your story; and
2. discuss reasons for choosing or not choosing each of the two possible endings.

Dear Jack,

I am unsure which ending I should choose for Robinson Crusoe Here they are in short detail. Number one goes something like this

The footprint that Robinson found was from a search party that was looking for him. There was only one because the tide came in overnight and washed the others away. The search party was wandering the island looking for him. They find him and he is rescued.

The End

The second goes like this:

It is the same up until the part where the search party rescues him. Instead of rescueing him, the wander the island, can't find him, and leave without him. They saw his things and knew that Robinson had been there, but thought that maybe he made a raft (he is a resourceful guy) and was trying to drift home. He ends up dying on the island.

response continues

Annotation for MEDIUM Writing Model • Rhetorical Effectiveness: Score 3

This response presents the situation clearly but briefly. The letter proceeds to describe two possible endings. The proposed endings are both reasonable, and there is limited development of each ending. The strongest element of the response is the attempt to speculate about the effects of the two endings ("I am leaning with the first one because people hate to see a sad ending"). However, to earn a higher score, the response would have to present more elaborated, reasoned, and persuasive arguments.

(annotation continues on next page)

I am unsure which ending will be best I am leaning with the first one because people hate to see a sad ending. Also, he did all that work and it would be wasted if he just died. Thanx for your advice in advance

Sincerely,

BIG Dan

Annotation for MEDIUM Writing Model • Conventions: Score 3
The response is marginally successful at using the conventions of written language. It is flawed by missing punctuation, shifts in verb tense, and other errors. Some of the errors are disruptive to the reader.

Time to Write

Imagine that you are Daniel Defoe and are trying to finish your novel *Robinson Crusoe*. Write a letter to Jack Singleton, your friend and publisher, that does two things. Your letter should

1. speculate about two different possible endings to your story; and
2. discuss reasons for choosing or not choosing each of the two possible endings.

> Dear Jack,
>
> This is how I would end story I would let the foetsteps be from a tribe member. the member would found him and take him back to tribe leader. they would help he find his way back home or wherever he came from. or you can end it where he meets a woman that's been stuck on the island too. Where he wouldn't be so lonely. Thank you for listening to my comment for the story. That is just my opinion.
>
> Thank you again,
> Roberta Hayes
>
> P.S.
> What ending do you like the best? Write me back soon!

Annotation for LOW Writing Model • Rhetorical Effectiveness: Score 1

The writer of this response begins abruptly, showing little regard for the reader. The letter briefly presents two possible endings but provides few details and very little elaboration. There is no speculation about the effects either ending would have on readers and no arguments (logical or otherwise) for either ending. Instead, the writer reveals a lack of confidence about her or his speculations (i.e., "That is just my opinion").

(annotation concludes on next page)

Annotation for LOW Writing Model • Conventions: Score 2
The response exhibits very limited ability to use the conventions of written language. Although the response is comprehensible, to fully understand it, the reader must supply missing words and mentally correct other errors in verb tense, sentence structure, and pronoun usage.

ASSESSMENT • 3

READING: POEM/JOURNAL, EXCERPT
WRITING: REFLECTIVE ESSAY
(EXPOSITORY)

Responding to the Selection

Now that you have read the poem and journal entry, respond to the following items as completely as possible.

1. Take a few minutes to write down your first response to the poem and journal entry.

After reading the selections my first response was to reread the poem. Wordsworth's poem appeals to me more than does his sister's journal entry because it elicits greater emotion from the reader. By placing himself in the piece as a part of nature, rather than a separate observer, Wordsworth makes the work much more interesting and meaningful. Again, I believe his message is more insightful and inspiring than Dorothy Wordsworth's; the daffodils he witnessed years before have made more than a fleeting impression on him. While his sister seems to observe their beuty within a beutiful scene, William Wordsworth has been affected by their greater implications. They almost seam to strike a chord within him; in their isolation from the stars, clouds, and sea these yellow flowers are carefree and peaceful. Such are the sensations William Wordsworth experiences as he views the daffodils in his minds eye.

response continues

2. In the space below, sketch or describe images from these readings that are especially memorable or significant for you.

SKETCHES AND DESCRIPTIONS

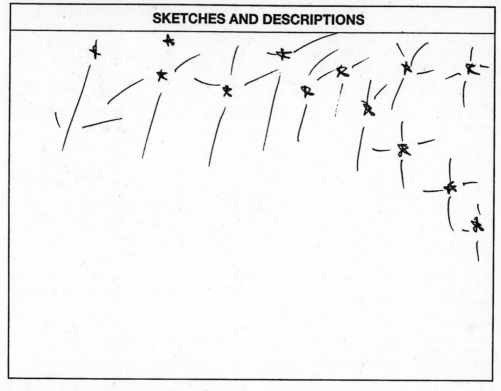

Explain why you chose these images.

"... the stars that shine / and twinkle on the milky way / " — It's interesting that Wordsworth chose to include such distant, isolated bodies in his work. One might not immediately picture stars when dreaming of daffodils, but I think the connection is valid. The stars he mentions may be the daffodils of another world far away.

response continues

3. Think about the following quotations and complete the questions in the chart below.

QUOTATION FROM THE TEXT	LITERAL MEANING: WHAT IS THE WRITER SAYING?	PERSONAL RESPONSE: WHAT DO I THINK OF THE IDEA?	REFLECTIVE RESPONSE: WHAT DOES IT SAY ABOUT THE WORLD?
"I gazed—and gazed—but little thought/ What wealth the show to me had brought:"	as he first saw the flowers, Wordsworth didn't realize the view would affect him years later	I think it's an important distinction—we often cannot comprehend the magnitude of a sight until it has remained w/us	rather than take nature for granted, we should open ours minds to the future effects its beauty may have on us
" . . . some rested their heads upon these stones as on a pillow for weariness and the rest tossed and reeled and danced and seemed as if they verily laugh-ed with the wind that blew upon them over the lake, they looked so gay ever glanc-ing ever changing."	the flowers almost seemed to have a personality—human characteristics. they were unconcerned w/ other beings	I don't think too much of the passage—I prefer William Wordsworth's view of the flowers as massive and isolated yet alive	everyone (every being) has different personalities and marches to a different tune

After you have filled in the chart, write one or two sentences explaining how you think William's and Dorothy's reflections on the flowers are different from each other.

William views the flowers as affecting the external world while Dorothy seems to see them as solely w/in their own realm of nature, having little effect on others

response continues

4. What do you think William Wordsworth means when he writes, "I wandered lonely as a cloud"? Why does he compare himself to a cloud?

He, like the cloud, feels isolated and distanced from the world. Like the cloud he has a view of nature and can view it in the larger scope. A cloud is fleeting — ever moving across the sky and always changing shape and form, much like man himself.

response continues

5. Create the first line of a poem in which you do what William Wordsworth does in the first line of his poem—compare a part of your life to something in nature. Then, explain why you chose that image from nature to say something about yourself.

Like a crab I creep cautiously in the dark—
a crab can hide within itself to protect
itself. It must live in the
blackness of the ocean floor—not
always able to see where it
is going or where it came from.

response continues

6. Use this page to write down any additional thoughts you have about the poem and journal entry. Tell anything else about your understanding of the selections and what they mean to you.

I still feel as I did in the first question, but I have greater respect for Wordsworth's poem - his analogy to a cloud is really insightful and realistic. I'm inspired by the lesson he drew from a patch of ordinary flowers.

Annotation for HIGH Reading Model • Score 6

This is a perceptive and insightful response. In responding to the first item, the student compares the two selections and steps outside the poem to make some evaluative judgments about the authors' craft. Virtually all of the responses reveal reflection and a search for deeper meaning. The responses in Item 3 visibly demonstrate this reader's progression from literal understanding to personal reaction to reflective response. Throughout, this student exhibits both emotional and intellectual engagement with the selections.

Responding to the Selection

Now that you have read the poem and journal entry, respond to the following items as completely as possible.

1. Take a few minutes to write down your first response to the poem and journal entry.

The poem and journal were very calm, and they seemed very peaceful. The poem allowed my mind to become more at ease, than the journal did. The journal and poem gave a thorough description of the flowers and it was almost like I could actually see the glorious features of the flowers. I felt as if I were actually experiencing the sight first hand.

response continues

2. In the space below, sketch or describe images from these readings that are especially memorable or significant for you.

SKETCHES AND DESCRIPTIONS

poem:
When he saw the daffodils dancing and tossing their heads.
When the daffodils out danced the waves
And when his heart will pleasure was filled and it to danced with the daffodils

journal:
The daffodils rested their heads up on the stones as on a pillow for weariness
The lake had floated the seeds ashore and that the colony of daffodils had sprung up.

Explain why you chose these images.

Because they were the ones who actually made me fell as if I were in the poem, and journal watching the daffodils first hand.

response continues

3. Think about the following quotations and complete the questions in the chart below.

QUOTATION FROM THE TEXT	LITERAL MEANING: WHAT IS THE WRITER SAYING?	PERSONAL RESPONSE: WHAT DO I THINK OF THE IDEA?	REFLECTIVE RESPONSE: WHAT DOES IT SAY ABOUT THE WORLD?
"I gazed—and gazed—but little thought/ What wealth the show to me had brought:"	He didn't need a T.V. to see amazing things he could just walk right outside a view nature.	I agree, people today do tend to view more material things than the beautiful things of nature.	The world today looks more at the views of material things and less at the things of nature.
"...some rested their heads upon these stones as on a pillow for weariness and the rest tossed and reeled and danced and seemed as if they verily laughed with the wind that blew upon them over the lake, they looked so gay ever glancing ever changing."	Maybe the flowers had died and fell over on the stones.	I liked it. I felt as if he were trying to say even though the flowers had died there was no need for life not to go on.	When people die, life still has to go on. So focus on the people we still have not at the ones who have gone.

After you have filled in the chart, write one or two sentences explaining how you think William's and Dorothy's reflections on the flowers are different from each other.

William looked at the flowers for companionship.

Dorthy looked at the flowers for mere pleasure.

response continues

4. What do you think William Wordsworth means when he writes, "I wandered lonely as a cloud"? Why does he compare himself to a cloud?

There is hardly ever only one cloud in the sky at a time. Like clouds, he was not the only man on earth, but he didn't have anyone to comfort him, and neither does the clouds.

response continues

5. Create the first line of a poem in which you do what William Wordsworth does in the first line of his poem—compare a part of your life to something in nature. Then, explain why you chose that image from nature to say something about yourself.

I felt as happy as a tree being hugged by the ornaments at Christmas.

Because after reading the poem it made me happy and as if I wasn't alone, like a tree probably does also feel happy when it is being decorated by the ornaments because it knows it is not alone.

response continues

6. Use this page to write down any additional thoughts you have about the poem and journal entry. Tell anything else about your understanding of the selections and what they mean to you.

I know now when ever I feel alone
I don't need a T.V. or radio to feel
comforted, all I have to do now is walk
right outside.
The journal and poem means a lot
to me it has made me change my
views about nature.

Annotation for MEDIUM Reading Model • Score 3
This student exhibits some engagement with the selections. For example, the initial reactions to Item 1 stress the aesthetics of the poem and how it made the reader feel, and the response to Item 6 reveals the student's "new" view of nature. Also, the student does a respectable job of modeling the first line of the poem in Item 5. However, the overall response lacks the thoroughness and deeper understanding found in higher-scoring papers.

Responding to the Selection

Now that you have read the poem and journal entry, respond to the following items as completely as possible.

1. Take a few minutes to write down your first response to the poem and journal entry.

My first ~~to~~ response ~~was it yea~~ to the journal and poem I jist read is that they look beyond all the problems in this world and pay attention to all the little things in life like how beautiful the flowers look on a windy day.

response continues

2. In the space below, sketch or describe images from these readings that are especially memorable or significant for you.

SKETCHES AND DESCRIPTIONS

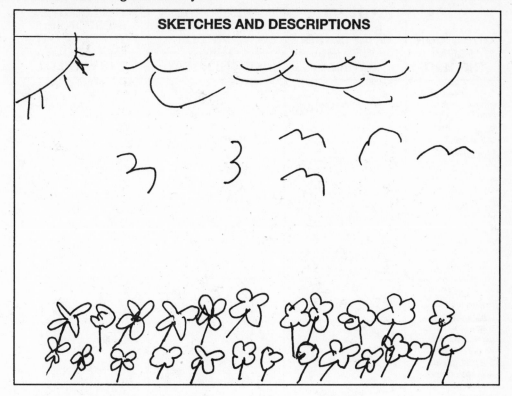

Explain why you chose these images.

this is the first image I
pictured when I read the
poem I pictured a lot of
flowers on a sunny day
blossoming and looking
really beautiful

response continues

3. Think about the following quotations and complete the questions in the chart below.

QUOTATION FROM THE TEXT	LITERAL MEANING: WHAT IS THE WRITER SAYING?	PERSONAL RESPONSE: WHAT DO I THINK OF THE IDEA?	REFLECTIVE RESPONSE: WHAT DOES IT SAY ABOUT THE WORLD?
"I gazed—and gazed—but little thought/ What wealth the show to me had brought:"	he wasn't thinking about anything just looking at how beautiful the flowers look.	I would think exactly how the writer is thinking	the world has a lot of beautiful thing to offer.
" . . . some rested their heads upon these stones as on a pillow for weariness and the rest tossed and reeled and danced and seemed as if they verily laughed with the wind that blew upon them over the lake, they looked so gay ever glancing ever changing."	the flowers looked peaceful and happy	I don't know what else to think because I see it the same way.	the same as the first one.

After you have filled in the chart, write one or two sentences explaining how you think William's and Dorothy's reflections on the flowers are different from each other.

I don't think they are different I think they are thinking the same they are just expressing thereselves diffently.

response continues

4. What do you think William Wordsworth means when he writes, "I wandered lonely as a cloud"? Why does he compare himself to a cloud?

He could GO ANYWHERE HE WANTS TO GO ALL HE HAS TO Do IS Put HIS MIND TO IT AND HE CAN DO ANYTHING AND GO ANYWHERE ▲ YOU NEED TODO IS USE YOUR IMAGINATION AND YOU COULD GO ANYWHERE

response continues

5. Create the first line of a poem in which you do what William Wordsworth does in the first line of his poem—compare a part of your life to something in nature. Then, explain why you chose that image from nature to say something about yourself.

I dont know any lines to a poem. He wondered lonely as a cloud. He went wherever His mind Took Him in 'His IMaginatin that what His First line is saying.

response continues

6. Use this page to write down any additional thoughts you have about the poem and journal entry. Tell anything else about your understanding of the selections and what they mean to you.

I dont really like poems so I dont get anything from them. The poem I just read I understood what He was tring to explain. That poem was O.K. The journal entry I didn't under much of it But there isn't much to understand in a journal writing because it is your own thoughts so it doesnt matter what anyone else thinks.

Annotation for LOW Reading Model • Score 1

This student displays very limited understanding of the selections. The student does grasp some literal details but never develops a deeper interpretation of the selections. In Item 3, the student exhibits difficulty differentiating the "literal meaning" from a "personal response" or a thoughtful interpretation. The student's inability to move beyond a strictly literal interpretation is also apparent in the response to Item 5, in which the student fails to write an original line of poetry. Responses to the final item ("I don't really like poems"; "there isn't much to understand in a journal writing") are characteristic of low-scoring papers.

Time to Write

You have been asked to write an essay for your school newspaper. The essay should have a philosophical tone—that is, it should describe a commonplace experience or object and then reflect about what that experience or object reveals about a particular aspect of growing up. You do not have to convince your readers that you are "right." You will simply be sharing your ideas and trying them out in an exploratory way. You may want to start by describing the everyday experience or ordinary object. Then explain what the experience or object reveals about growing up.

One summer several years ago, I was on my porch when all of a sudden I saw a bird's nest in a hanging fern of ours. I saw the mama bird bring twigs and leaves to make the nest a home for her family.

The days passed on and every now and then I would peek to see how mama's four little eggs were doing. My mom and I kept a close watch on the nest to make sure none of the eggs fell out or were disturbed.

Then one day, my birthday, I went to look at the nest and three little birds were craning their skinny necks and crying for food. I was so happy to see them and they shared the same birthday as me.

As the days past, I saw the mama bird feed and love her newborns. Unfortune- ately, the fourth egg never hatched and was disgarded by the mother.

response continues

I watched the babies grow and get feathers, I was so proud. I felt like their mother sometimes, always making sure they were o.K. The funnest part was watching the mama teach the babies to fly. It was so cute to see them try so hard and drop, but they never quit and their mother always supported them.

Not too long afterwards, they were gone. In that short time they had grown up enough to be able to take care of themselves. They no longer had the security of their mother or the nest. They had to fend for themselves.

It's funny how much we learn from our parents just so we can leave them when we grow up. Then we pass those same things onto our children so they can leave us someday.

I am now getting prepared to go out on my own at college. I know I will be responsible for my own actions and I can't go back to my mother to

response continues

Annotation for HIGH Writing Model • Rhetorical Effectiveness: Score 6
In this response, the student presents an extended and detailed experience. The student also includes several reflective statements (e.g., "It's funny how much we learn from our parents just so we can leave them when we grow up"). Although the response lacks the exceptionally fresh and original insights usually found in the very best papers, the authenticity and the generally high quality of the observations and reflections merit a score of 6.

(annotation continues on next page)

help me. We spend the first part of our lives learning. Then we must let go so we can teach others what we have learned and also try out what we have been taught. My mother has cared for me and taught me how to fly. Now I must do it on my own and teach it to others.

Annotation for HIGH Writing Model • Conventions: Score 5
The response demonstrates successful use of the conventions of written language. A few minor mechanics and spelling errors are evident, but the errors do not interfere with communication.

Time to Write

You have been asked to write an essay for your school newspaper. The essay should have a philosophical tone—that is, it should describe a commonplace experience or object and then reflect about what that experience or object reveals about a particular aspect of growing up. You do not have to convince your readers that you are "right." You will simply be sharing your ideas and trying them out in an exploratory way. You may want to start by describing the everyday experience or ordinary object. Then explain what the experience or object reveals about growing up.

The most ordinary incident that I can think of – and one that almost every teenager goes through sometime in their life, is getting their drivers' license. It gives you freedom, by allowing you to be in charge of yourself. A great deal of responsibility will suddenly be bestowed upon you! And most importantly – a teenager with a drivers' license will begin to realize that in a few years, they will be an adult, and life is passing them by very quickly.

When a teenager gets their license, they suddenly become a new, free person. They have the choice to do what they want, and go where they want – when they want to. That is – if they are lucky enough to have a car! There's no more calling parents, asking for a ride home, or to school, or to the mall, you're on your

response continues

own. You will be able to go out with your friends - free from the hassle of waiting around for parents to show up. It's a great feeling, and on the day you walk out with your license - every teenager should know that their life is changing right before their eyes - and a whole new sense of maturity is beginning.

Getting a license is definitely an ordinary situation that everyone goes through in their life. But once the first few "days of glory" are over, after you get your license, every 16-year-old must realize that a whole new sense of responsibility is beginning, also. You suddenly become in charge of yourself. You are in charge of all your own actions, and you pay the consequences. It's a sort of responsibility that signals the beginning of growing up to be an adult.

Most people are fortunate enough to get their license when they are 16, and for some, it doesn't signal a

response continues

Annotation for MEDIUM Writing Model • Rhetorical Effectiveness: Score 4

This response presents a commonplace experience (getting a driver's license) and offers several reflective comments. However, the reflective statements are very general and predictable (e.g., "It gives you freedom, by allowing you to be in charge of yourself"; "It's a sort of responsibility that signals the beginning of growing up to be an adult"). Although this student has developed the response reasonably well, the paper lacks the specific details, keen insights, and convincing reflection found in stronger responses.

(annotation continues on next page)

change. But for most teenagers, a new sense of freedom, responsibility, and maturity has begun, and one should realize that they will be an adult soon, and its something to look forward to, and be happy about. Responsibility, maturity and freedom acquired when one gets their license shows that life is changing, and with it, so should we.

Annotation for MEDIUM Writing Model • Conventions: Score 3
The response demonstrates some evidence of achievement at applying the conventions of written language. However, the paper contains several errors in usage and mechanics, which tend to disrupt the meaning of the response.

Time to Write
You have been asked to write an essay for your school newspaper. The essay should have a philosophical tone—that is, it should describe a commonplace experience or object and then reflect about what that experience or object reveals about a particular aspect of growing up. You do not have to convince your readers that you are "right." You will simply be sharing your ideas and trying them out in an exploratory way. You may want to start by describing the everyday experience or ordinary object. Then explain what the experience or object reveals about growing up.

Getting good grades in school is important when growing up. Some people like to goof off a bit and then their grades start slipping and then they fail. Like me I was a straight A student from first grade till the fifth grade then I got lazy and started goofing off and then my grades started slipping and I barely graduate out of the eighth grade. Now I am barely making it through high school.

So it is important to get good grades in school because then you get smarter and then you get a better job and make more money. And if you want to get into a good college you need very good grades.

Annotation for LOW Writing Model • Rhetorical Effectiveness: Score 1
In this response the writer only vaguely presents an occasion for reflection ("... I was a straight A student from first grade till the fifth grade then I got lazy and started goofing off ..."). What little reflection the writer does present is extremely general, predictable, and simplistic ("So it is important to get good grades in school because then you get smarter and then you get a better job and make more money").

Annotation for LOW Writing Model • Conventions: Score 2
The response displays very limited ability to use the conventions of written language. The paper contains several usage and mechanics errors, and the errors make the response somewhat difficult to read.

ASSESSMENT • 4

READING: AUTOBIOGRAPHY, EXCERPT
WRITING: INFORMATIVE REPORT
(EXPOSITORY)

Responding to the Selection

Now that you have read the autobiographical passages, respond to the following items as completely as possible.

1. Take a few minutes to write down your first response to the autobiographical passages.

My first response was one of enlightenment. Vera Brittain brought up some areas of life in World War I that I did not know about. Her life as a nurse was a hard one to live. She spoke of the raids, panic, and casualties as if they were an every day thing. It was not only her war life that interested me, it was her war life as a woman. She explained the mental, as well as physical, conflicts she experienced. Her family life was just as important as the war and she would have to choose. It was much easier for her brother, for he was not expected to stay home.

response continues

2. In the box below, use words, pictures, or symbols to show how Brittain felt after she read her father's letter.

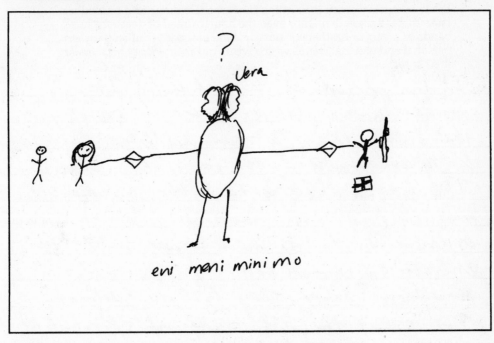

Now explain why you chose these words, pictures, or symbols.

In this picture, Vera is being pulled
from opposite sides. On one side, her
parents are pulling her home, and on
the other side, the war effort is pulling
her to war. The question mark and the
statement "Eni meni minimo" ~~can~~ represent her
inability to make a decision.

response continues

3. In the space below, give your opinion of what Vera Brittain means by the following statement:

> What exhausts women in wartime is not the strenuous and unfamiliar tasks that fall upon them, nor even the hourly dread of death for husbands or lovers or brothers or sons; it is the incessant conflict between personal and national claims which wears out their energy and breaks their spirit.

In the period of World War 1, women were still expected to stay in the home. Many women accepted that, yet, every one should fight for their country. This is the excessive task that women must deal with in wartime. Women were expected to do so much more and their energy is drained trying to accomplish those tasks. When they fail to complete those tasks, the lose pride and spirit like any normal human would.

response continues

4. Brittain implies that the experience of serving one's country during war differs greatly between men and women. In the following chart, report your conclusions about how Brittain sees these differences. The chart also has a space for you to include your opinions about how men and women experience war.

	BRITTAIN'S THOUGHTS	MY THOUGHTS
Men in Wartime	Their path is clear. They must serve their country, That is it. It is duty. There is no effort to make a decision. It has been made for them.	Men were irresponsible in a certain point of view.
Women in Wartime	There path is very clouded. They are torn between two worlds. There are more than one duties and obligations. They have to be involved in the home and war. One cannot be neglected.	The time period made it somuch tougher for the women. Even though, there are still problems of this sort today. for a while, women will have to deal with this until all of society changes

response continues

5. Use this page to write down any additional thoughts you have about the autobiographical passages. Tell anything else about your understanding of the passages and what they mean to you.

I wonder how it was for other women in the war. Did all women have the same difficulty in deciding between obligations? It is discouraging how men could have been so overbearing and irresponsible. They took no responsibility for their actions in neglecting the family and don't attempt to make it right. Women should not have been forced to carry such responsibility.

Annotation for HIGH Reading Model • Score 6

This response displays intellectual engagement with the reading selection. Much of the interpretation focuses on the special burden that women carried during World War I. The sketch in Item 2 is an excellent pictorial representation of the conflict the author was experiencing. Not only does this student grasp the major theme in Brittain's selection, she or he is able to place the author's dilemma in a historical context and contrast it with current times ("In the period of World War I, women were still expected to stay in the home": Item 3). The question that the reader raises in response to Item 5 shows that the selection served as a springboard to deeper thinking about the issues and the times.

Responding to the Selection

Now that you have read the autobiographical passages, respond to the following items as completely as possible.

1. Take a few minutes to write down your first response to the autobiographical passages.

It made me think of what it would be like if I was there. Excellent choice of words. Instead of afraid they used panic-stricken and frantically. They showed not only what was happening there but at home. The details and the vocab used made it very readable and interesting. I felt like I was there

response continues

2. In the box below, use words, pictures, or symbols to show how Brittain felt after she read her father's letter.

Now explain why you chose these words, pictures, or symbols.

She was upset that her family was hurt, but felt that it was her duty to stay and help fight.

response continues

3. In the space below, give your opinion of what Vera Brittain means by the following statement:

> What exhausts women in wartime is not the strenuous and unfamiliar tasks that fall upon them, nor even the hourly dread of death for husbands or lovers or brothers or sons; it is the incessant conflict between personal and national claims which wears out their energy and breaks their spirit.

She means that when there are conflicts with family, and there are national tragedies, she doesn't know which to choose. She feels that she has to remain loyal to her country but also wants to reman loyal to her family.

response continues

4. Brittain implies that the experience of serving one's country during war differs greatly between men and women. In the following chart, report your conclusions about how Brittain sees these differences. The chart also has a space for you to include your opinions about how men and women experience war.

	BRITTAIN'S THOUGHTS	MY THOUGHTS
Men in Wartime	She thought that men had no problem Killing people.	~~I don't think the~~ I think that men have an easier time Killing people than women because ~~a~~ men want to win
Women in Wartime	Women thought more about who they were killing.	Women are more likely to think of their families.

response continues

5. Use this page to write down any additional thoughts you have about the autobiographical passages. Tell anything else about your understanding of the passages and
what they mean to you.

It was very easy to read. The vocab & details
made it easy to picture myself there.

Annotation for MEDIUM Reading Model • Score 3

This student displays some engagement with the text and an appreciation of the author's craft
("Excellent choice of words"; "The details and the vocab used made it very readable and interesting. I felt like I was there": Item 1). Item 2 reveals a limited understanding of the author's
dilemma, although this understanding is enhanced in the response to Item 3. The explanation
of gender differences (Item 4) is simplistic. Overall, this response is a fairly literal interpretation
of the text with some flashes of insight.

Responding to the Selection

Now that you have read the autobiographical passages, respond to the following items as completely as possible.

1. Take a few minutes to write down your first response to the autobiographical passages.

A worried nurse in a hospital wants to take a long time off because off the bomb-threat going on in her country. She is having flashbacks of the mess she stayed in.

response continues

2. In the box below, use words, pictures, or symbols to show how Brittain felt after she read her father's letter.

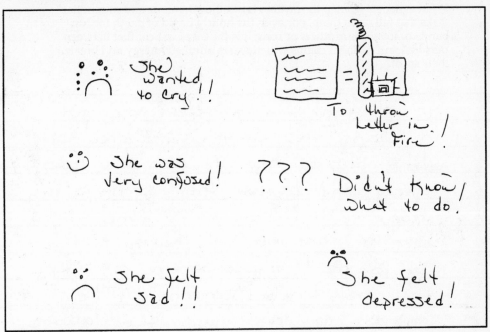

Now explain why you chose these words, pictures, or symbols.

She wanted to cry.
She wanted to throw the letter in a fire.
Her emotions were very strong. ...
She didn't know what to do after she
read the letter. She was very confused
with herself and her thoughts.

response continues

3. In the space below, give your opinion of what Vera Brittain means by the following statement:

> What exhausts women in wartime is not the strenuous and unfamiliar tasks that fall upon them, nor even the hourly dread of death for husbands or lovers or brothers or sons; it is the incessant conflict between personal and national claims which wears out their energy and breaks their spirit.

All their time and effort they put in during the wartime. I agree with Vera because how she says she loses energy and breaks their spirit is very true. They take a lot time in the war to help men if they're hurt. It is hard to see someone go after they have helped someone. Their spirits go down and they loose their energy after someone has passed away. The reason they are there is to help the hurt and sickness and to make them feel better.

response continues

4. Brittain implies that the experience of serving one's country during war differs greatly between men and women. In the following chart, report your conclusions about how Brittain sees these differences. The chart also has a space for you to include your opinions about how men and women experience war.

	BRITTAIN'S THOUGHTS	MY THOUGHTS
Men in Wartime	How men and women react different	
Women in Wartime	~~How women take feelings harder and~~ How women get depressed easily and loose their spirits.	

response continues

5. Use this page to write down any additional thoughts you have about the autobiographical passages. Tell anything else about your understanding of the passages and what they mean to you.

I didn't exactly read the
section good enough to tell about the
passage.
   — I know it's about women in wartime.
   — Britian receives a letter from her
      father.
   — She doesn't know what to do.
   — or how to react.
   —

Annotation for LOW Reading Model • Score 1
This paper displays no major misconceptions, but the student focuses on parts of the text only and does not develop an interpretation of the entire selection. This is most evident in the response to Item 5. Here, the student lists events from the passage but does not tie them together. The sketch in Item 2 also reflects this partial interpretation. Virtually no evidence of reflective thinking or engagement with the text is evident throughout the response.

Time to Write

Write a report of information for your social science teacher in which you describe a conflict of obligations that people have experienced. In your report, do not take sides in the conflict. Instead, concentrate on clearly describing the nature of the conflict you have chosen to write about. Include examples from personal experience, from news reports you have seen or read, or from the lives of fictional characters in books, TV, or films. Present an objective report on the problem and try to make your report informative and engaging.

John is a lawyer at a major firm. He makes a great deal of money, but doesn't have much free time. or family time. He figures he'll have plenty of time for that after he retires. His family consists of 3 people besides himself; a daughter who's 7, a son who's 5, and a wife. They live in a nice city, subdivision and house, but John's wife thought something in their life was lacking. She knew it wasn't money, but she just couldn't place her finger on it. In a society based upon social standing it is hard to decide if your loyalty goes to your employer or your family.

An employer is a person in which one works for. Through your employer you receive paychecks; and with your paychecks you purchase things you want or need. It's a mutualistic relationship. Once you buy the things you want or need people, other than your family, see

response continues

these things. If they are materialistic,
your "social standing" is raised. Your
family is then thought of as being "good
enough" for whomever is the judge. Its
then become cylical in that once you start
climbing you don't want to fall; so
you put in more hours at work which
causes your family to grow apart.

Families are very important. They give
you a sense of belongingness, love, and
commitment. When in a family, you
need to spend time together and work
together as a group. If one person
doesn't care and share in the work
then they will fail. Many families within the
U.S. today are being broken up by divorce.
People aren't making the same effort that
there was before in preserving relationship
w/each other and their families. Time is
what is needed to do this.

John isn't working as much anymore
because he realized his commitment to his
family is just as important as his work.
Was he wrong before, it's a matter of
values and opinions. What is important
to one man or woman may not be to

response continues

Annotation for HIGH Writing Model • Rhetorical Effectiveness: Score 5

This response is a clearly written and interesting report about the conflict between career and family. The writer employs various strategies, such as the opening scenario about a lawyer, in order to describe the nature of the conflict. The response includes some specific insights into issues such as social standing and divorce. The response contains some flaws (e.g., shifting points of view, awkward sentences, obvious information), but overall the writer is involved with the subject and displays an authentic voice.

(annotation concludes on next page)

to another and vice-versa. In a
society based upon social standing
it is difficult to decide where your
loyalty should be, to your family or
employer.

Annotation for HIGH Writing Model • Conventions: Score 5
The response generally demonstrates successful use of the conventions of written language. A few minor flaws in usage, mechanics, and spelling are evident, but the errors do not interfere with communication.

Time to Write

Write a report of information for your social science teacher in which you describe a conflict of obligations that people have experienced. In your report, do not take sides in the conflict. Instead, concentrate on clearly describing the nature of the conflict you have chosen to write about. Include examples from personal experience, from news reports you have seen or read, or from the lives of fictional characters in books, TV, or films. Present an objective report on the problem and try to make your report informative and engaging.

Many people experience a conflict of loyalties in today's world. One such conflict that many people experience is the conflict of having fun versus doing your work. Below I will describe both sides of the conflict.

One side of the conflict, is having fun. It's natural to want to have a good time. Many people will choose having fun over working, but which one is really more important.

Some people, decide to do their work before they have fun. This way the work is done, and completed on time, and then they can go out and have fun knowing they have completed their work. Instead of the people who have fun, who leave their work to be done late, or incomplete.

It all depends on which is more important to you. Some people think fun is more important than work, but others think that work comes before having fun.

An ~~Exmp~~ Example of this, is many kids today. They have to choose between going out and having fun, or staying home and doing

response continues

Annotation for MEDIUM Writing Model • Rhetorical Effectiveness: Score 3

This response reflects some evidence of achievement. The paper contains a reasonable amount of information, but the information is not specific or interesting. The writer states an obvious position and provides no relevant insights (e.g., "Some people think fun is more important than work, but others think that work comes before having fun"). In summing up the paper, the writer frankly acknowledges, "This is a very small conflict . . ."

(annotation concludes on next page)

their school work. Some kids even do both, in the same night, but others just go "out", or do their work.

Many people can also influence other peoples choices. Your teachers ~~one~~, coaches, or bosses can make you do work over going out. And most of all, your parents ~~are~~ or family can ~~I~~ influence your decision.

This is a very ~~I~~ ~~~~~ small conflict, but many people face it every day. And it is a tough decision to make.

Annotation for MEDIUM Writing Model • Conventions: Score 3
The response is generally clear and readable. However, there are numerous minor mechanics errors. In addition, some usage errors disrupt the meaning of the response. Overall, the response demonstrates marginally successful use of the conventions of written language.

Time to Write

Write a report of information for your social science teacher in which you describe a conflict of obligations that people have experienced. In your report, do not take sides in the conflict. Instead, concentrate on clearly describing the nature of the conflict you have chosen to write about. Include examples from personal experience, from news reports you have seen or read, or from the lives of fictional characters in books, TV, or films. Present an objective report on the problem and try to make your report informative and engaging.

I have seen a conflict with two parents and how they argue about stupid things, like when the parents argue about money for the house. They argue what money go's for what and what money pays bills. They get into a big figut because one parent wants to spend money on something and the other parent dosn't and say's they need it for something else and it never work's out

Annotation for LOW Writing Model • Rhetorical Effectiveness: Score 1
This response reflects minimal evidence of achievement. The writer presents the subject briefly with minimal elaboration. The "report" does not include many specific details, convey information accurately or convincingly, or establish the writer as an authority on the subject.

Annotation for LOW Writing Model • Conventions: Score 1
Although the response is very brief, it contains several errors in usage, mechanics, and spelling. The incorrect use of apostrophes is a glaring weakness (i.e., "go's," "say's," "work's").

FIELD-TEST SITES

Alvord Unified School District
Riverside, California

Armona Union School District
Armona, California

Escondido Union School District
Escondido, California

Fowler Unified School District
Fowler, California

Fresno Unified School District
Fresno, California

Kings Canyon Unified School District
Reedley, California

Mattoon Community Unit #2
Mattoon, Illinois

Metropolitan School District of Decatur Township
Indianapolis, Indiana

Middletown Public Schools
Middletown, Connecticut

Mobile County Public Schools
Mobile, Alabama

Montgomery County Public Schools
Rockville, Maryland

Oakfield Alabama School District
Oakfield, New York

School District of Palm Beach County
West Palm Beach, Florida

School District #200
Wheaton, Illinois

Sweetwater Union High School District
Imperial Beach, California

Weber County School District
Ogden, Utah

Winslow Township Schools
Cedarbrook, New Jersey